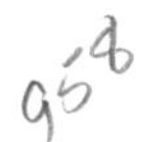

Additional Praise for
Life, Liquidity & the Pursuit of Happiness

"During my 30 years at IBM, I wished I had a book to hand to my team that explained equity awards in plain English. If you're serious about looking after your employees, give them this book on day one. They'll get a valuable financial education—stock options, RSUs, taxes, investing, and risk are all discussed in plain English—and you'll get a knowledgeable and grateful team."

—Mark Fantacone, Retired IBM Software Manager

"Joyce Franklin's *Life, Liquidity & the Pursuit of Happiness* makes a very valuable contribution to the understanding of how to optimize wealth. While chiefly focused on the wealth that can be created—and perhaps lost—through participation in startup ventures, the key insights apply to any situation where hard work, creative energy, and at least a little luck produce opportunities for making the most of personal wealth. Franklin brings her insights close to home through many interviews with people and advisors on the front lines of significant financial success. Entrepreneurs, employees, advisors—and students of human psychology—will quickly relate to the stories of smart planning and missed opportunities, and can readily grasp the lessons that Franklin often entertainingly draws from them."

—Tim Kochis JD, MBA, CFP®

Founder and Former CEO and Chairman, Aspiriant

Board of Directors, Financial Planning Standards Board

Board of Trustees, Charles Schwab Strategic Trust-CSIM

"Business school is part one. *Life, Liquidity & the Pursuit of Happiness* is part two. An indispensable resource for holding on to what you made."

—Jamis MacNiven, Restaurateur/Investor, Proprietor of Buck's of Woodside

"No one ever talks about their own money in Silicon Valley. That's why this book is so crucial. Joyce Franklin gets executives and entrepreneurs to go on the record about how to hang on to hard-earned wealth."
—David Weinfeld, Engineer, Marketing Executive, and Entrepreneur

Life, Liquidity & the Pursuit of Happiness

How to Maximize and Preserve
Your Startup Wealth and
Live Your Dreams

Joyce L. Franklin, CPA, CFP®

Rubydon Press

Publisher's Cataloging-In-Publication Data

Franklin, Joyce L.
  Life, liquidity & the pursuit of happiness : how to maximize and preserve your startup wealth and live your dreams / Joyce L. Franklin, CPA, CFP.

   pages : illustrations ; cm

  Issued also as an ebook.
  Includes bibliographical references and index.
  ISBN: 978-0-9916172-0-3

  1. Businesspeople—Finance, Personal. 2. Liquidity (Economics). 3. Wealth. 4. New business enterprises—Finance. I. Title. II. Title: Life, liquidity and the pursuit of happiness.

HG179 .F73 2014
332.024

For permission to reprint, and for bulk-order information, contact Info@RubydonPress.com.

Cover design by Randle Design.
Interior design by Ponderosa Pine Design, Vicky Vaughn Shea.

RUBYDON PRESS
Larkspur, CA

To my clients, and to those creating and building companies.

CONTENTS

INTERVIEWEES

Samuel N. Adler
Director of Global Demand Generation, Zuora, Inc.

John Bowen
CEO, Financial Advisor Select, LLC
CEO, CEG Worldwide LLC

David Buchanan
Former Manager of Asia Pacific, Extreme Networks

Roy Bukstein
CFO, MMM Management
Former CFO, Oracle

Lise Buyer
Principal and Founder, Class V Group

Ed Callan
Owner, Callan Consulting
Project Faculty, Wharton Global Consulting Practicum

Jonathan Cardella

CEO, NeighborCity®

Former CEO, OTravel.com, Inc., D/B/A Overstock.com Travel

Robert M. Carter

Principal, RMC Development

Former SVP of Content and Business Development, NuvoMedia, Inc.

Mitch Cohen

Former Managing Director, Hellman & Friedman LLC

Stephanie Coutu

Partner, Arnold & Porter LLP

Edward Deibert

Partner, Arnold & Porter LLP

Lara Druyan

Founding Partner, G&B Partners

Vice Chairman of the Board of Trustees, City of San Jose Retirement System

Martin Eberhard

Founder and Former CEO, Tesla Motors Inc.

Leland Fong

Former Senior Network Architect/Project Manager, Inovant (a subsidiary of Visa Inc.)

Eliot Franklin

Principal Engineer, Entropic Communications

Mark E. Galant

CEO, Tydall Trading

Founder, GAIN Capital

Rachel Garb
Designer & Manager, Google

Eric Gold
Sales Director, Couchbase

Ken Goldman
CFO, Yahoo
Former CFO, Fortinet (during the IPO)
Former CFO, Siebel Systems
Former CFO, Excite@Home Network (during the IPO)

Jason Graham
Managing Director, WTAS

Peter Herz
CEO, WUCO Capital, LLC
Co-Founder and Former CEO, 3ware

Michael Irvine
Partner, Gunderson Dettmer

Darrell Kong
Former Director of Venture Capital Services, Fenwick & West

Jim Koshland
Partner, DLA Piper

Danny Krebs
Partner, Alliance Counsel LLP

Jamis MacNiven
Owner, Buck's of Woodside

Dee Anna McPherson

Vice President of Marketing, HootSuite

Lesa Mitchell

Vice President of Innovation & Networks, Ewing Marion Kauffman Foundation

Marlee Myers

Managing Partner, Pittsburgh Office of Morgan, Lewis & Bockius LLP

Rob Nail

CEO & Associate Founder, Singularity University

Co-Founder and Former CEO, Velocity11

Lee Pantuso

CFO, NeoCarta Ventures

CFO, CMEA Capital

Sonja Hoel Perkins

Managing Director, Menlo Ventures

Richard Pivnicka

Honorary Consul General, Czech Republic

Member of the Board of Directors, Gerson Bakar & Associates

Former VP and General Counsel, Gerson Bakar & Associates

Joe Preis

CEO, Longitude Properties, Inc.

Former CEO, MetroRent

Brendan Richardson

Co-Director, Galant Center for Entrepreneurship, McIntire School Foundation at the University of Virginia

General Partner, Northface Ventures

Laura Roden
Founder, Capital Formation Consultants, LLC
Former President & CEO, Silicon Valley Association of Startup Entrepreneurs (SVASE), now known as SVForum

Stephen Roth
CEO, Carmel Software Corporation

Jeff Russakow
CEO, Findly
Former Executive VP and Chief Customer Officer, Yahoo!

Alexandra Derby Salkin
Vice President for Philanthropic Services, Marin Community Foundation

Santosh Sharan
VP of Product Management & Strategy, ZoomInfo
Founder and Former CEO, Keisense, Inc.

Tiffany Shlain
Founder and Director, Moxie Institute Film Studio + Lab
Founder, The Webby Awards

David Spark
Founder, Spark Media Solutions, LLC

David Stern
CFO, Greenberg Brand Strategy

Marc Tarpenning
Founder and Former VP Electrical Engineering, Tesla Motors Inc.

Nicolai Wadstrom
Founder, BootstrapLabs

Rebecca Weeks Watson

VP of Business Development, RadiumOne, Inc.

Bill Weihl

Manager of Energy Efficiency and Sustainability, Facebook

Mark Cameron White

Partner, White Summers Caffee & James LLP

Bruce Wilford

MTS, Graphite Systems, Inc.

Former Distinguished Engineer, Cisco

Sylvia Yam

VP of Business Development, Sincerely

Former Director of Business Development, Tiny Prints, Inc. and Shutterfly

Some interviews were conducted in confidentiality, and the names of those interviewees are withheld by mutual agreement.

PREFACE

OUR MEDIA LANDSCAPE IS FILLED WITH TALES of people who work hard, build innovative businesses or awesome technologies, then go through a rewarding IPO or sell to deep-pocketed corporations. But with a few notable exceptions—early eBay employee and Academy Award–winning producer Jeff Skoll, Microsoft founder and humanitarian Bill Gates, the "Google masseuse"—we rarely hear the details of what happens to their money after their windfall events. What's more, this silence goes both ways: so many of the lucky folks who go through liquidity events are unwilling or uncomfortable talking about their experiences, and sensible, unbiased advice about what to do with these fortunes—paper, stock, or cash—seems hard to come by. Some insiders even go so far as to suggest that people who might go through a wealth event shouldn't do any planning before the money is in hand or the options are vested. I strongly disagree with this notion.

When my husband sold his software company in 2008, I realized how few resources exist to help executives and employees manage the financial challenges of a liquidity event—the sale, merger, or initial public offering (IPO) of a company you work for or own.

I'd been helping clients through sudden-money events for nearly 15 years as a CPA and CERTIFIED FINANCIAL PLANNER™, but it wasn't until the sale of my husband's company that I learned the emotional side of a liquidity event firsthand—including the excitement, negotiation, realization it might not happen, and finally the completion of the transaction.

While the deal with Autodesk, a large 3D design, engineering, and entertainment software company,[1] was all cash, and my husband's net worth was not tied to the acquiring company's stock price, he did have a contractual obligation to remain at the company. Thus, Autodesk's financial statements—which he did not control and hardly could influence—were now important to our family's future. I also learned the emotional impact that a dip in the stock market can have after a recent, very large, investment. Applying emotional detachment to the investment enabled me to secure the long-term value of our portfolio. This was a great opportunity for me to put into practice several smart financial planning moves.

In January 2008, we invested the first and largest tranche of my husband's (after-tax) sales proceeds in the stock market. Fate then took an interesting turn. Beginning that summer, the broad stock market started to plunge; it was the start of the Great Recession, and the market was melting. Between the summer of 2008 and the bear market low on March 9, 2009,[2] I reviewed our investment portfolio often to "harvest" and realize the losses we had from the market's drop. Selling one position and buying a similar but not identical holding to retain market exposure is what I do anyway for my clients during market downturns.

Although the proceeds from my husband's decade of hard work lost one-third of their value during those 15 months between when we invested them and the bear-market low, grabbing those tax losses turned out to be hugely helpful to our personal 2008 and 2009 tax bill. During this time, I had successfully preserved—or realized—losses of an amount equal to approximately 30% of the cash he invested in January 2008. We essentially used these losses to offset the gain from the sale of his company. This is a really big deal, and it bears repeating. My execution of our investment management strategy reduced the tax bill on the sale of my husband's company by 30%.

As of this writing in August 2014, returns from the broad stock market (using the Russell 3000 Index as a benchmark) have recovered from the 2008 plunge.[3] While the stock market has returned to its pre-bear-market level, the silver lining in the bear market for us was that realizing the losses meant that our portfolio offset the gain on the sale of my husband's company, dollar for dollar, against the losses I harvested! Not only did he pay less tax on the sale of his company, but the clincher here is that our portfolio retained exposure to the stock market throughout the turbulence. Over that five-year period, we maintained our principal and the exposure to the stock market we need to meet our long-term goals.

The stock market is a volatile place, and you can be sure that every few years your portfolio will suffer a loss. While we hope we will never again see a bear market like the Great Recession, our experience made my husband realize the value of professional advisors. Before he met me, he considered most advisors to be the unskilled equivalent of "vacuum cleaner salespeople," but he changed his mind when he saw that my smart planning moves had a big impact on our family's future.

Our shared experience riding out the startup life cycle of building and selling a company and the Great Recession, along with my decades of wealth planning experience and expertise, make me uniquely qualified to provide crucial information to others about how to increase personal wealth via strategic opportunities that exist in the world of high tech. Furthermore, I conducted more than 65 interviews with leading high-tech entrepreneurs, executives, and notables who share their insights. My findings—along with my own observations—are all in this book.

Life, Liquidity & the Pursuit of Happiness is about your money AND your life. You'll learn how to protect and preserve your hard-earned wealth through smart financial and tax planning strategies that are specifically focused on stock options, restricted stock, and a financial windfall that may be a once in a-lifetime event. This book also tackles the "What's Next?" phase that comes after a corporate exit.

This book sprouted from my husband's experience into the idea that I could help the high-tech community. It is a resource guide to help tech executives and employees make smart financial decisions.

Joyce L. Franklin, CPA, CFP®

INTRODUCTION

A FEW YEARS AGO, I HAD TWO CLIENTS who worked for a hot telecommunications company that went through an initial public offering (IPO). After taxes, each wound up with more than $3 million in vested options in their company's stock. As their financial advisor, I formulated specific plans for each to diversify. We discussed verbally and in writing the importance of selling some of their stock options to diversify their net worth. But despite my imploring, the only selling these paper millionaires did was just enough to buy and remodel homes.

As they rode the company's stock on a roller coaster from less than $10 per share, up to over $200, and back down to nearly $0, they hoped and prayed the stock would go back up, but they *never sold*. Finally, with a permanently low stock price, the company changed its name. My clients were left with worthless stock options and modest (remodeled) homes. Neither had contributed any of the windfall toward retirement, wealth accumulation, or other life goals.

I took their inability to diversify personally.

As the personal CFO for my clients, I'm not going to let this happen again. In my 20 years as a wealth planner, I love that I've helped so many people enjoy their lives and achieve their dreams. But those two high-tech clients still give me pangs of regret. I feel like I let them down. And it didn't have to be that way.

This story, in which sudden-money individuals or IPO lottery winners ride their potential riches down to zero—or worse, lose their money on expensive purchases or by failing to plan for taxes—is all too common in the high-tech world and Silicon Valley, in particular. It's easy to go astray or become paralyzed without a guidebook to help navigate the complexities, challenges, and choices involved in a wealth event.

This is that guidebook.

Over more than two years, I conducted upwards of 65 interviews with leading entrepreneurs, high-tech executives, and notables in order to find out what it takes for personal financial success in all stages of launching, building, and exiting a startup. Some sources are humble people who shun the spotlight but spoke as a favor to me or to a mutual friend. All have deep insights to share with you. Many of my sources were happy to go on the record. Others were eager to protect their privacy and only felt comfortable discussing sensitive topics if I did not identify them by name.

This book is organized into sections based on the Four Phases of Startup Life (see chart on page 3): The early days of a startup in Phase 1, ramping up to a liquidity event in Phase 2, a brief chapter on liquidity events, the post-event period in Phase 3, and retirement or other ventures in Phase 4. While executives and early employees often move on to Phase 4 once they've accumulated enough wealth (which might be through one large or several modest events), entrepreneurs typically never transition to Phase 4; instead, they return to Phase 1 after each exit. Financial planning and tax tips are sprinkled throughout the book, and helpful checklists for addressing your personal finances are included at the end of each chapter for quick reference.

It's easy to assume wealth planning starts only after a liquidity event. However, as I explain throughout this book, windows exist early on in the life of a company that allow you to make decisions that could affect your net worth in a big way. After the event, new and surprising challenges appear. Having insight about what lies ahead is crucial for making good decisions.

Whether you're a recent college graduate starting at your first tech company or a seasoned executive, understanding and planning around the Four Phases of Startup Life can help you make smart financial decisions about your personal wealth. If it's your job to educate others in your company, or if you are an advisor or investor wanting an insider's look at Silicon Valley startup culture, this book will be a great resource to help you understand the tech world.

For entrepreneurs, unique challenges and financial planning opportunities are explored in detail in my book *Startup Wealth: The Entrepreneur's Guide to Personal Financial Success and Long-Term Security.*

The Four Phases of Startup Life[SM]

Phase 1	Phase 2	Liquidity Event	Phase 3	Phase 4
Pre-Transition 2-40 years Laying the Foundation	**Pre-Transition** 0-24 months Ramping Up		**Post-Transition** 1-24 months Realizing the Dream	**Into the Future** 2-40 years What's Next?
Quality of Life Challenges				
Preoccupation with startup Loneliness Optimism Tenacity	Maintaining balance while working long hours Excitement Persistence		Weighing career options If you stay: Vest in peace and maintain work-life balance If you leave: Figure out what's next	Flexibility and choices Charitable activities Travel New career or startup Passion projects
Financial Challenges				
Raising capital Below-market salary Accountability to investors Funnel all resources to create and build the company	Increasing enterprise value Salary and bonus Accountability to investors, management, and board Planning with equity awards		Increasing enterprise value and stock price Accountability to shareholders, board, and management Diversification of concentrated position Expensive purchases	New or second home Venture or angel investing Strategizing goals with financial resources

Common to All Phases

Challenge	Maximize Value of Equity Awards (ISO, NQ, RSA, RSU, ESPP)
Concerns	Wealth Preservation Tax Reduction Wealth Protection Passing Assets to Heirs Charitable Giving
Solutions	Personal CFO Expert Team of Advisors Financial Education

The Four Phases of Startup Life

Here is a brief introduction to each phase.

PHASE 1: LAYING THE FOUNDATION

For executives and employees, the months or years you spend building and growing your company are very exciting. It's during this time that you get your team together and identify your product or service. You're also raising capital and may take a below-market salary.

Many people are preoccupied night and day with their startup, even to the point of sleeping at—or under—their desks because they can't stand being away from their work. This phase can also be very lonely and filled with doubt. A female executive at a well-known Bay Area tech company who experienced multiple wealth events said that each time she was in Phase 1, she had no social life.[1] Instead of spending time with friends, all of her time and energy were devoted to building her company and raising her son.

PHASE 2: RAMPING UP TO THE LIQUIDITY EVENT

For the lucky few who manage to work at—or start—the right company at the right time, a big wealth-creation event—an IPO, a sale, or a merger—is a once-in-a-lifetime happening. For an even luckier few, lightning may strike twice or three times. It's important to realize early on the ramifications of what you do with an equity award.

LIQUIDITY EVENT: THE PAYOFF

This is the time you've been waiting for. You and your team have received tangible financial proof that your company is valuable. Depending on which type of liquidity event you go through, what you experience in Phase 3 can vary.

PHASE 3: REALIZING THE DREAM

The two years following a company's liquidity event can bring on many changes. These changes can be big, like a reorg—as likely in a merger or company sale as in an IPO situation—or so small that you hardly notice them. The day-to-day routine may stay the same, but that startup, we're-all-in-this-together feeling usually fades. While Phase 3 can bring a great sense of appreciation and fulfillment, some find their workdays much less interesting, and much more routine.

PHASE 4: INTO THE FUTURE—WHAT'S NEXT?

After the heady startup days have passed and the euphoria of sudden wealth brought on by your liquidity event has faded, a different kind of excitement unfolds: you get to decide how you want to live the rest of your life—and how to make sure you can afford it.

PHASE 1
LAYING THE FOUNDATION

Pre-Transition Phase
2–40 Years

The Four Phases of Startup Life[SM]

Phase 1	Phase 2	Liquidity Event	Phase 3	Phase 4
Pre-Transition 2-40 years **Laying the Foundation**	**Pre-Transition** 0-24 months **Ramping Up**		**Post-Transition** 1-24 months **Realizing the Dream**	**Into the Future** 2-40 years **What's Next?**

Quality of Life Challenges

Phase 1	Phase 2	Phase 3	Phase 4
Preoccupation with startup Loneliness Optimism Tenacity	Maintaining balance while working long hours Excitement Persistence	Weighing career options If you stay: Vest in peace and maintain work-life balance If you leave: Figure out what's next	Flexibility and choices Charitable activities Travel New career or startup Passion projects

Financial Challenges

Phase 1	Phase 2	Phase 3	Phase 4
Raising capital Below-market salary Accountability to investors Funnel all resources to create and build the company	Increasing enterprise value Salary and bonus Accountability to investors, management, and board Planning with equity awards	Increasing enterprise value and stock price Accountability to shareholders, board, and management Diversification of concentrated position Expensive purchases	New or second home Venture or angel investing Strategizing goals with financial resources

Common to All Phases

Challenge	Maximize Value of Equity Awards (ISO, NQ, RSA, RSU, ESPP)
Concerns	Wealth Preservation Tax Reduction Wealth Protection Passing Assets to Heirs Charitable Giving
Solutions	Personal CFO Expert Team of Advisors Financial Education

LAYING THE FOUNDATION

GORDON MOORE AND ROBERT NOYCE founded Intel in 1968, when they saw the potential to use microchips for data storage and computer memory.[1] Engineer Andy Grove had worked with both founders at Fairchild Semiconductor, and as often happens when brilliant founders start a company, loyal colleagues follow. Grove joined Intel to be part of their revolution, without even having an official job offer. He was soon on the executive team, helping the company solve the particularly tough problem of how to get lots of memory onto a tiny computer chip.

In a 2012 interview with NPR, Grove recalled day-to-day startup life: "Every pestilence that could kill a microchip hit it." Of the team's experiments to develop low-cost memory on a chip, he said, "We had no idea what we were doing. Key people [were] standing around and testing all the chips in a wafer: 'Green light is good,' 'Red light is bad.'" The days were long, but the years were short. After two years—which felt like 20 to Grove—they unveiled a working chip.

Grove has always believed a company should be built to last by creating a product and business of value. He cringes at the phrase "exit strategy" when he hears young tech entrepreneurs and VCs use it in reference to starting a company with the goal of getting rich and getting out.

"I really don't have much respect for the people who live their lives motivated by an exit strategy," he said. "There was no option that we were trained in that says, 'If it gets too hard, get up and leave.'"

Intel was formed out of a passion to solve a problem. The executives didn't think about liquidity during the early years when they were growing their close-knit team. Through hard work and preparation, enormous wealth eventually came as a benefit of their success. Early employees worked hard to make the company a leader at a time when there were 50 other semiconductor startups. Their tenacity paid off. "We're about the only ones still around," Moore said in the interview.[2]

With too few people doing too many things, working at a startup these days—as in the early days of Intel—can be really exciting, and really hectic. Most people have the patience and the stamina to be in a startup for a few years, after which they generally either ramp up toward a liquidity event or rethink their motivation for staying. Phase 1 is the time to improvise with scarce resources and "work like hell through chaos." For this phase, I explore the challenges startup employees and executives face in choosing the right startup, maintaining work-life balance, understanding compensation packages and equity awards, and, for some, determining when it's time to jump ship.

Startup Life

As he reminisces about his first job out of college, serial entrepreneur and Carnegie Mellon graduate Peter Herz describes the difference between working in a large corporation and working in a startup, and how his experience differed from that of his college classmates.[3] "A bunch of my friends joined very big companies, and I went to a startup on the East Coast," he remembers. "In keeping up with my friends over that first six to 12 months, the ones that went into big companies were basically put at a desk, given a stack of documentation multiple feet high, and told to study it for the next six months." At Herz's startup, "We had a half day of orientation, and by the afternoon of the first day I was designing stuff that was going to go into a product. I've always, ever since then, really enjoyed startups and small companies, because you always have too few people, and that means you end up doing things you haven't done before. What gets me out of bed in the morning is learning. That's my motivation. The people who are rational about this type of pursuit understand that it's not about an economic outcome."

Software sales executive Eric Gold says this about his first position in a startup: "It was my first experience with having real autonomy. The autonomy was the most exciting thing about it. When you're young and you're just starting out, you hear people talking about an IPO, but you don't really know what it means. The whole process is unfamiliar. So it was just more fun to be a part of a growing business where people are trusting me to run my own show and do my part."[4]

Phase 1 was the most challenging stage for Roy Bukstein, who counts serving as the CFO of Oracle among his many high-profile Silicon Valley jobs.[5] "I didn't know how I was supposed to do it, so I did it during the IPO by the seat of my pants." Like most startups in Phase 1, cash was short, he remembers. "I strung out vendors. I robbed Peter to pay Paul. We did whatever it took to run the company in those days." Like many startup folks, Bukstein left Oracle in Phase 3, within two years of the IPO. "Pre-IPO we had to count pennies," and it was exciting, he notes. "Post-IPO, it was staid." The company spent lots of money, there was greater accountability on the part of the executive team, and in Bukstein's view, things were just not as interesting.

PRE-LIQUIDITY STRESS

The time before a liquidity event can be very stressful. Not only are you building the product, but you also have to build the company, and you have to raise money for it—all at the same time. The work is super exciting, but the hours are tremendously long. "It's also utterly manic-depressive," says Tesla founder and serial entrepreneur Marc Tarpenning.[6] "There are days where you realize, 'Wow, we're going to be larger than Microsoft!' Then the next day, you think, 'We're never going to get this out. No one is ever going to give us money.' It's tremendously exciting, tremendously fun. But from a health perspective, it's less than ideal."

And if you get investor funding—either angel or VC—you have added stress, due to new investor accountability. That seat-of-the-pants way of doing business may have to go by the wayside in favor of the more traditional business practices that investors prefer—and even insist on.

Loneliness can be a problem during Phase 1, and several entrepreneurs spoke about hiring coaches to deal with it. Perhaps the biggest personal challenge in a startup environment is maintaining balance, a quest which drives some people out of the tech industry. "People are giving up the money and the opportunity to live a healthier lifestyle,"[7] says an interviewee who requested privacy and was working in sales at a prominent technology company when we spoke. "Not every company is fun and cool and [headed for] a home run—most companies are not. This is high-pressure, long hours, intense, mission-critical hardcore stuff. And it's not always fun, and it's not always glamorous. Even if they're making really good money and have lots of stock in a company," he notes, "some people are just going to say 'this isn't worth it, I want to move to South America.'"

While you're building a great company, "make sure to spend time with family," advises Bukstein, who is currently CFO of MMM Management. "Time goes by fast and you can get seduced," by the money. "It often takes an event to shock you to step away from work." In Bukstein's case, it was the death of his close friend and co-founder of Oracle, Bob Miner, at age 52 from nonsmoker's lung cancer. After Miner's death, Bukstein sold his interest in his CPA firm, where he had given stock option advice to hundreds of startup employees, and went to work for the Miner family business, a commercial property development company in San Francisco.

> "The secret to avoiding burnout: be on a mission that doesn't suck."
> —Tweet from Aaron Levie, CEO at Box, Inc.[8]

POSITIONING YOURSELF FOR A JOB AT A STARTUP

Your business reflexes and instincts are built in your 20s and 30s, so the companies and industries you choose early on create the framework for your future.

Former marketing executive Dave Buchanan had two strategies for acing a job interview and understanding the corporate culture.[9] First, he "got the [interviewer] talking more than I talked." And second, "You want to get them talking about company myths." In other words, don't ask canned interview questions if you want to find out what makes a company tick.

Buchanan told a story to illustrate. Early in his career at Hewlett-Packard, he worked in the marketing department. The office consisted of desks pushed together in a big room, where it was customary to answer colleagues' phones if they weren't around. (This was in the dark days before voice mail.) "It's like 5:30 at night, and executives are walking down the aisle next to this four-foot-tall partition. A phone starts ringing over in marketing, and the VP of Marketing swings his leg over, essentially hurdles the barrier, goes over, and grabs the phone." That story illustrates what the VP of Marketing thought was important, and told you what he would do to get a sale, to succeed, Buchanan remembers. "It's those kinds of stories you want to hear, particularly about executive actions. 'Tell me a funny story about your exec. Has he done anything funny or quirky lately?'"

DEVELOPING YOUR HUMAN CAPITAL

For fresh college graduates, compensation at a startup may not be too different from compensation at a more established company, but you can expect greater opportunities to develop your human capital. One interviewee remembers, "Right out of college I started working for a startup media company founded by an Internet pioneer."[10] Through that connection, this source got to meet many of the founders of companies that would later explode in success. "It was a really great experience for me and helped me build my network and my skill set." These intangibles acquired early on can help your résumé and set you up for future success—a form of compensation, if you think about it, especially if you're just starting out in your career. "With anything in Silicon Valley, your personal network is your best resource," says this ambitious high-tech employee.

Founders and early employees in a startup should understand what their real risk is, according to Bukstein. "To spend $5,000 to exercise your stock options is a big risk. But there's a bigger risk: that you are in the wrong company!" You waste five years of your human capital if you stay at the wrong company for five years. The moral is to love your job and continually be learning, though you should also have long-term confidence about your company. "Life is like a spreadsheet," says Bukstein, who is also a CPA. "We are the sum of our experiences. The values of the spreadsheet's cells are different sizes, and circular formulas don't make sense. The fuller your spreadsheet, the better life you've had."

A NOTE ON COMPENSATION

If you join a startup, you're working for the learning experience and a big payout through the appreciation of your stock options or other equity awards, not for great benefits or a high salary. If you're laid off, severance will be nonexistent. If you value high compensation today, don't work at a startup.[11]

> ## NEGOTIATING FOR EQUITY
>
> An engineer with 25 years of experience in startups with varying degrees of success says he wishes he had negotiated for more options in his early days.[12] He acknowledges, "At the time, I didn't have the experience to do it differently. As a non-founding engineer, I figure [I could have asked for] about 1% of the company. That's not an unreasonable starting point." He clarifies that this percentage is for a senior engineer in a company with 15 to 30 employees.

A SANDWICH AS A SALARY

After working for others for 12 years, Peter Herz started his company in 1997 and personally bankrolled it with his co-founder. "The compensation plan at that point was if you came to work we bought lunch, and if you stayed late we bought dinner," he says. There was also equity, but no salary. Their team was "very eclectic," composed of people the co-founders knew who were between projects. "We talked to a number of people who were intrigued with the idea of joining a startup." However, "it is a very sobering moment when you put a $0 offer letter on the desk." It was clarifying to remove salary from the equation. "I had a number of people who did not join at the time because, for some, it didn't make sense, and for other people, it wasn't the right time in their lives, [or] in their careers, to make that kind of step. If you've got a family, you can't do that."

Herz and his co-founder ended up with a very dedicated group of people at 3ware. Working collaboratively with a fierce belief in the company's product, the team's optimism fueled its expectations for a financial payoff. The employees were betting their human capital on equity, rather than salary. And the gamble paid off well for those who got in early.

"We hired a buddy of mine out of Netscape, a very, very talented software developer," Herz recalls. "When we made the $0 offer letter, it took him a while to come around to the decision, but he decided to jump. When he resigned [from Netscape], he went through the entire executive team at Netscape, and everyone tried to retain him; it was a very interesting path, all the way to the top. Each one of them tried to keep him, but then in telling their own stories, talked about the point where they had to jump ship from some big safe place and dive into some crazy startup." The developer's eyes were opened and he made the leap. "Despite their stated intention of trying to convince him to stay, [the Netscape executives] ended up making it really clear that if you really want to go out and do something, you need to take a risk at some point. And so he watched what they did rather than what they said."

In the end, "He joined us, and that was great. We built a small team of committed, potentially insane people."

Real Wealth Versus Paper Wealth

Bukstein believes "real wealth is having at least $5 to $10 million." And working at a pre-IPO company is the only way to earn this kind of money, unless you are a top executive at a successful company. To clarify, he explains, working at the *right* pre-IPO company may be your one and only shot at earning real wealth. If you are relatively young and have accumulated a few million dollars, your planning decisions are even more important, and with a net worth of less than $5 or $10 million, you'll be working again one day.

Independent marketing consultant Ed Callan, the then VP of Global Marketing at a company that went IPO during the dot-com boom, emphatically believes everyone, especially young tech workers, should be saving now for the future.[13] In-the-money equity awards "may be their one-time bump" in net worth. Sadly, Callan saw young people take no action to sell their options after his company's IPO, "because they think of it as 'free money,'" he remembers. "Easy come, easy go is the mindset because they got it for 'free.'"

Callan adds that a financial advisor can help "young people figure out what their future looks like." While he acknowledges that buying a toy with stock proceeds is fine, as someone who has made smart decisions after his own IPO event, he wisely advises others to "take 80% of your net profits from the [equity] sale and look at long-term investments to secure your financial future."

A LITTLE BIT OF LIQUIDITY

CPA Jason Graham has seen some tech executives get surprised in Phases 1 and 2.[14] "While they're private," says Graham, "and as they're going through rounds of financing, it's become a trend where the founders of the company want to get some cash off the table. They'll present their case to the board and say, 'Look, you know, we're barely getting by. I'm living out of an apartment. I'm riding my bike to work. I'm eating Top Ramen. It'd be nice to get a little bit of liquidity. I'm not talking about totally cashing out, but just a little bit of liquidity so I can live a little bit more comfortably and recognize some of this value.' The problem is," Graham continues, "the founders generally have common stock, and the people coming in buying into the company, they don't want common stock. They want preferred stock."

Money, Pre-Liquidity

The world has changed for early employees. Today, says Marc Tarpenning, "We've all learned" from the mistakes of the dot-com, over-concentrated days. For example, he says, at "Groupon, all the investors and a bunch of the original employees had already pulled out all the money they had put in the company before the IPO, which was unheard of 10 years ago. People [were] trading shares in Facebook for three years prior to the IPO. There's a lot of people in Facebook who have sold hundreds of millions of dollars' worth of [pre-IPO] shares in the secondary markets. This is new." Tarpenning won't speculate on the effect this change will have on people's personal net worth but says, "It used to be, until the day of liquidity, everyone was trapped" in the company's illiquid stock. The early liquidity available today changes the game—or at least the opportunity for wealth—significantly.

One of the reasons for the advent of this new secondary market is that going public is much more expensive than it was 15 years ago. An IPO now comes with more regulatory challenges, as well. Instead of going public in four years, it could take eight. The team must buy more time and look for ways to get founders and employees more cash. What's a tax-efficient way of doing that? How do you minimize dilution to the overall enterprise? The answer, more and more, is to have team members sell some of their stock back to the company.[15]

If you're lucky, you'll have guidance from your company or a proactive executive team member about how to optimize the long-term impact of your company stock. Read the story of one such helpful executive, Kate.

THE TEAM-PLAYER EXECUTIVE: KATE

SERVED AS IN-HOUSE ATTORNEY AT MANY STARTUPS
AND THROUGH THREE LIQUIDITY EVENTS.

Kate (not her real name)[16] is a self-proclaimed "deal junkie." She told me, "There's something about the excitement of putting together a deal, knowing that you built the company to the point where it's either going public or being acquired. It's the realization of what you've built."

Through all three of the acquisitions and the one IPO she has been a part of, Kate has always been exceptionally concerned about the executive team and employees who helped to build the company to the point of a liquidity event. Her goal is to ensure that the team benefits from its years of hard work. As an executive and general counsel, Kate takes it upon herself to educate employees about equity and trading rules so that they can make smart decisions with the wealth created at the company: "Making sure that people are taken care of is my biggest concern, because a number of employees may not understand what the financial consequences are going to be to them personally, post-acquisition."

Her passion for helping her team and providing knowledge to the high-tech community at large prompted her to accept my interview invitation, even though she did not want her name to appear in print.

Education Before and After Liquidity

As an in-house attorney, part of Kate's job at the startups she's worked for has been educating employees about the legal and tax ramifications of a liquidity event. "You can just see people's eyes glaze over. In a public company you have education responsibility, especially about insider trading." Most concerning, when Kate explains the specifics of exercising stock options to employees—including the tax consequences—"I don't think people get it. When I was working at one dot-com in the '90s, people got hit with huge tax bills. They exercised options and held them, and then the value of the stock went down so much that the tax consequence for all the employees together was about $11 million, when the stock was worth nothing" at the point when the tax bill was due.

"They were naïve," with their options, Kate recalls, "because everybody thought things would continue to go up. Some people had remodeled their house and couldn't pay for it. Some had to sell their house. A lot of people made ill-advised decisions, especially in that era. Part of the struggle is that you can't treat employees like children if they're making senseless decisions, but you want them to be educated."

One solution is to bring in a professional financial educator to explain the general rules of stock options to employees. However, Kate cautions about the lack of customization in these talks. She recalls prior to her starting at one dot-com, "they brought in a financial advisor to talk to employees. But the advisor was really pushing insurance policies, and a lot of people went with it. I thought that was a mistake." A problem with captive brokers is that employees may not realize they're missing out on truly comprehensive planning. Only a wealth planner with fiduciary duty is going to provide the kind of unbiased advice you need for success.

Competing Interests in a Startup

Kate also described how as an acquisition becomes likely, often either the CEO or the general counsel will seek outside legal advice on behalf of the entire executive team. "Getting an executive comp person to review how your [contract] is structured is really important," Kate says. "If you don't already have these items addressed when you join, then at the point of an acquisition, the management team would benefit from having their own counsel on these matters, because there can be a split [in self-interest] with the board." Sometimes the investors want liquidity events for reasons other than what's in the company's best interest. For example, "Say a VC hasn't had a liquidity event in their portfolio, they may want to push an acquisition because they need that to validate themselves within their VC firm. There are all sorts of different reasons that can be a problem, but generally, premature liquidity events do not bode well for future success and growth. The management team really needs to look out for the company and themselves."

At a digital media company that was bought out in the mid-2000s, Kate experienced her third liquidity event. A few years earlier, the management team renegotiated its contracts with the board. "This is a timing thing," says Kate. "If you can, at the point when the company's sales are going through the roof or it looks like you might be an acquisition target, get the board to agree to put some sort of protective provisions in place for the executive team. It can be very beneficial. That's what we did, and everybody was covered at that point, in the event that something happened."

Take Action Sooner Rather Than Later

For the purposes of wealth enhancement in a company sale or merger transaction, Kate advises that in Phase 2, "right before an acquisition, it can make sense to exercise part of your options, and not the rest. Wait for the rest to convert [to stock of the new company]. Not only are there tax consequences on exercise—you're going to have to come up with the money to pay the taxes—but it can also take some of the risk off the table to not have your stock convert into the other company's stock." Due to vesting requirements on most deals, and escrow on others, her advice to people approaching a liquidity event is to "look at parsing up your holdings and dealing with them differently. It's usually a good idea, because it's diversification." Taking action with your stock options is not black or white, and it depends on your contract and the terms of the deal. At Kate's last acquisition, she explains, "What I did is to divide the options into different buckets, and have them treated differently, so I mitigated my risk.

"Executives in an acquisition situation can be very misled," cautions Kate. "In Phases 1 and 2, you have to be very aware of how the deal is structured and how things will play out post-acquisition. When the company is acquired, you sometimes have an executive team that has not fully vested in their stock." In her opinion, answers to the following questions can affect the personal financial position of each executive team member:

- Does the executive team get acceleration?
- Does the board get acceleration?
- Do the executives have to stay with the company for a certain period of time post-acquisition? And if so, what are the work responsibilities during that time?
- Is there compensation for staying post-acquisition?
- What are the terms of the escrow?

"With each deal, different things come up with each different company," says Kate. Different types of liquidity events also bring different challenges. In an acquisition, Kate's concerns for herself and her executive team are different than they would be were the company going through an IPO. In a public offering, the company is growing and continuing; the number of options and restricted stock granted will come into play a certain number of months after the IPO date (after the trading window opens).

From her unique vantage point, Kate has a strong sense of what's important. And what can go wrong. All the more reason to have an expert team of advisors on hand prior to the deal.

Finding an Attorney to Help the Executives

Surprisingly, Kate has yet to find many attorneys who really understand the issues important to tech executives going into a new company and who also work with individuals. "I've always found that I know more about some of the very technical employment contract issues than other attorneys." While she is fortunate to understand the issues, she'd like a second set of eyes to review her employment contract. The advisor must understand the accounting consequences on the options side, too, since there are so many ways to structure a deal.

What an attorney serving individual tech executives must

understand is "the reason people are in tech companies is you're taking a risk and you're doing it for the options, for the liquidity event, because in many cases, it's not the salary," Kate explains. "You're trying to build something to the point where there's value, and if you don't understand that that's the driving motivation, and it's not the salary and it's not the severance if someone is laid off, then you're not focused on the right things."

■ ■ ■ ■

Single and Double Triggers in an Acquisition

Having worked on mergers and acquisitions (M&A) at a large law firm early in her career, and as an in-house attorney working in the trenches on four liquidity events, Kate (see sidebar) has witnessed many high-tech deals go down. Her experience has given her unique insight regarding the legal issues executives and early employees are likely to encounter when joining a startup.

Negotiating to go into a company, it's important to understand what happens to your equity awards if there's a company acquisition or merger. A "single trigger" means all your stock options accelerate upon the change in control event. In reality, though, you're more likely to have a "double trigger" situation.[17] A double trigger is the acceleration of unvested shares based upon two events: an acquisition of the company and the employee's termination. When an acquisition or merger occurs, an employment agreement for a startup executive will generally address the following issues:

- Options vesting, in which a single trigger is preferred over a double trigger
- A gross-up cash payment to cover the tax liability if you're hit with the excise tax, or a restructure of your equity awards so that you don't get hit with the excise tax
- Severance payment, if you're terminated[18]

While it's more common to have a double trigger event upon a change in control, "how the double trigger is structured is really important," says Kate. "Say, they keep you on because they don't want to pay you, but you no longer have any of the same duties—you're basically just there so they don't have to accelerate your options, but you have nothing to do—that's not uncommon. Or they'll keep your title just so your options don't accelerate. You want to be sure that your employment contract is structured with a number of different triggers. [For example], even if there's a constructive termination [a situation in which an employee resigns because the employer's behavior is intolerable],[19] or the employee has a major change in duties post-acquisition, you can leave and your options accelerate."

UNVESTED EQUITY TRIGGERS

Here are two triggers that can cause acceleration of unvested equity.

❶ **Change of control**. For example, if the company is sold or merged. "You were CEO of your startup, but when Google buys you, you won't be CEO of Google. But if Google is buying your company, it's going to usually become a division. Then, you should still be head of that division or something close to it," says attorney Irvine.

❷ **Leaving the company**. There are different permutations, including if you leave the company or if you were fired (with or without cause, and how cause is defined). "If the company didn't fire you," says Irvine, but you got demoted "from head of sales to head of janitorial services, that's kind of a different job. Not what you signed on for. You're effectively fired at that point."

Emerging growth company attorney Danny Krebs of Alliance Counsel says the opportunity to resign for "good reason" should be included as one of the second triggers.[20] For example, if you have a reduction in salary or a material change in duty, resigning with good reason will get you the second trigger and preserve your equity awards.[21] Having an attorney read your employment contract is your best protection.

As he pounded the Phase 1 section of my Four Phases chart with vigor, startup venture capital lawyer Michael Irvine said Phase 1 is the best time to get acceleration of stock options written into your employment contract. These days, "boards have more discretion and flexibility over what happens to unvested equity upon change of control," he explained. "And now what we're seeing is boards actually have full carte blanche. Unless you have contractual acceleration [in which] it's written into your agreement, when the company gets bought, anything that's unvested could completely disappear into the ether."

Irvine knows of "hundreds of thousands of stories of that happening" and advises executives to push for contractual acceleration. "The VCs are focused on building liquidity to return money to their LPs [limited partners], so they want to maximize all of the talent value in the enterprise, build the enterprise value, get it sold or take it public, and get out. That doesn't jive with the founder who's trying to build up the enterprise, and who may want to take it to the next level, take it public, and hold on to it." Irvine noted, "The VCs have 100% acceleration. When the company gets bought, they're getting 100% liquidity." He advises founders and executives to fight for their rights in Phase 1, at formation. Irvine urges his founder clients to ask for 100% double trigger.

How Attorneys Can Help

Another reason to have an attorney is to play the heavy. Let's say you don't want to be perceived as too pushy, outspoken, or aggressive. Strategize with an experienced startup attorney about current deals and negotiate your contract directly with the founders or board. Or have the attorney negotiate on your behalf. This strategy is most effective if you present an aligned force and don't act as if your attorney is over the top with the demands, attorney Stephanie Coutu advises.[22] "No one will give you anything if you don't ask for it." However, it can be tricky to negotiate right before the liquidity event, since "a lot of that negotiation is really with the acquiring company."

Attorneys who understand issues at the heart of emerging companies can be helpful to the startup executive team. Look for an attorney who specializes in one or more of the following issues:

- Executive compensation and benefits
- Corporate emerging growth
- Technology transactions and intellectual property (IP)
- 409A and excise tax

One interviewee for this book said that finding competent attorneys to work one-on-one with executives is very tough, because most of the good ones are on the company side. The attorney you choose must understand the motivation for working in a startup, including a compensation structure based on stock options or equity, not salary. If you're having trouble finding one, ask an executive comp attorney on the corporate side to recommend a colleague who works with individuals.[23]

A STARTUP ATTORNEY: SETTING UP THE COMPANY FOR SUCCESS

LEGAL ISSUES FOR FOUNDERS AND EARLY EXECUTIVES.

Savvy startup executives think about how to minimize their risks. A good attorney can identify and frame the questions, and advise on how to set yourself—and your company—up for success.

Michael Irvine, a partner in the Silicon Valley office of Gunderson Dettmer, knows his niche. "About 75% of my practice is working with the companies and 25% is with the VCs." On the company side, his work focuses on formation, growth management, operations, raising capital, making introductions, and addressing issues that will affect both the company and its founders. One task he enjoys is giving "tough love speeches" to executive teams going through a liquidity event about how things work in the startup world, including the motivations of the other parties to the deal.

Contract Updates Before the Event

For executives who want to understand their rights or make some changes to their employment contracts right before the liquidity event, visit an attorney like Irvine. "In Silicon Valley, equity still is king," he says. Startup folks take below-market salaries early on and give up large severance packages when they join in return for an equity position and the hope of a future payout. "An executive coming into a publicly traded company may get 12 months' guaranteed severance, but for cash-strapped startups, even on the eve of an IPO, they still don't yet have that cash." VCs and other investors are always looking at how much cash a company has to get to the next milestone, whether it's raising new capital, getting the cash flow to break even, landing the next big enterprise sale to generate a bunch of cash, getting to an IPO, or getting a line of credit. "Having these guaranteed payments in place that sit on the financials and are open to view by other investors is not a good thing. [VCs] are really focused on preserving the cash position in the company."

But in Phase 2, if the company "is generating revenue and is close to cash flow positive, is it a huge burden for the company to guarantee you six months of severance?" asks Irvine. "I don't think so. I think you should be asking for that. That's on the cash side. And then on top of that, we'd layer in things like paying for COBRA benefits for at least the same period, if not 12 months. You've got to protect your family." Get a clear picture of what you have, and what your tax consequences may be.

Irvine also understands the dynamics of a changing organization: evolving from startup to acquisition target or public company. Part of his job is to help the executive team relate on a personal level. For example, he told one executive team just after an IPO, "I know you love this company, but now this is a public company. You are no longer the boss." He tells me a story about a VP of Finance who was excited for an upcoming acquisition payday but didn't yet realize he'd be out of a job. As a company advisor, Irvine looks out for the best interests of the company, but he often has very personal discussions with each founder individually.

■ ■ ■ ■

When Should You Exercise Your Options?

Jason Graham is a CPA who has been providing tax planning and compliance guidance to high-net-worth families in the Bay Area since 1998, the height of the dot-com boom. His specialties include stock option planning and small-business tax planning for entrepreneurs, venture capitalists, and executives.

He recommends employees exercise their options "as early as possible. It always makes sense, especially if they believe in the company. Usually, it's really cheap to exercise right when they get them. If they can do an early exercise,

exercise all of them." It's best to exercise early when there's no spread between the grant price and the stock's fair market value, and therefore no income associated with the exercise transaction. Early in Phase 1, the grant or exercise price could be 10 or 15 cents a share, and "usually they can afford to exercise all of them," says Graham. "They'll find the money to do it, because it's such a small investment." Borrowing from parents or a friend is a common way to get cash for this purchase.

If there is a spread between the grant price and the fair market value on the date of the exercise, says Graham, "there's going to be an income event on the exercise [date] if it's a non-qualified option, or a delayed tax payment if they have an incentive stock option. The difference between the two is if you [exercise] a non-qualified option, it's compensation and you have withholding tax on it right away. Usually the company will have you write a check to cover the withholding."

Exercising and holding can be risky. If your company never goes public, or if the stock price falls below your exercise price, you could lose all of the cash you paid to buy the shares. Exercise and hold shares only if you can afford to lose that cash. If you can't afford to lose the investment in your company's shares or you are financially conservative, hold no more than 5% to 10% of your net worth in shares of your company's stock. See the Financial Planning and Tax Tips section beginning on page 28 for details about planning with equity awards.

When to Jump off the Startup Ship

A senior engineer who started his career in the early days at a successful network equipment provider more than 25 years ago learned through experience how to tell if a company is on the fast track to failure. He says, "It's too easy to fall into the trap of thinking that [the startup you work for] is going to be [successful]."[24] At one startup, he remembers, "They went public, we had great engineering talent, but we didn't have a strong enough product. The company went public, but the stock never really went anywhere."

He was an early employee at three startups, each of which eventually failed. He remembers the absolute certainty that everyone on the team had about the future success, yet "emotionally, I ignored the fact that we weren't making as much progress in the product line as we should have been. It was woefully bad, because everyone was so sure they were going to be a bazillionaire, no one actually did any work. They came to work and discussed how rich they were going to be but didn't actually do much to progress the goal." Success relies on building a product, cautions the engineer. Among the red flags to watch out for: Are you getting the product built? Is the team focused on getting the job done?

The signs are clear to him now, he explains. Yet, when he was 25, his focus was on getting paid a salary and doing interesting work, and not so much looking out on the horizon toward his future security.

FINANCIAL PLANNING AND TAX TIPS

TIP 1 Equity Awards

Understanding your equity award inventory, and how each grant is taxed, can save you money and increase your wealth. To help demystify the process, below are some key terms. Throughout this book, I use the term "equity awards" to refer to stock options or restricted stock.

> **Incentive Stock Options (ISOs)**—Upon grant date, there are generally no tax consequences. Upon exercise, you do not recognize taxable income for regular tax purposes. However, the spread between the fair market value (FMV) on the date of exercise and the stock purchase price (the "bargain element") is taxable for alternative minimum tax (AMT) purposes. You must hold the stock for two years from the date of the grant and one year from the date of exercise to have a qualifying disposition. A gain on the sale of ISOs in a qualifying disposition is taxed at the favorable long-term capital gain rates. If you fail to meet the two holding period tests (two years from grant date and one year from exercise date), the amount by which the FMV on the date of exercise exceeds the strike price is treated as ordinary income, or compensation income, in the year that you dispose of the stock. Additional rules apply for disqualified dispositions of stock at amounts less than the FMV on the date of exercise and for disqualified dispositions that straddle two tax years.

> **Non-Qualified Stock Options (NQSOs)**—Upon grant date, generally there are no tax consequences. Upon exercise, you recognize ordinary income (generally subject to payroll taxes or self-employment taxes) to the extent that the FMV of stock on the date of exercise exceeds the strike price.

> **Employee Stock Purchase Plan (ESPP)**—If a company offers an employee discount, employees pay tax at ordinary income tax rates on the discount amount when shares are purchased, and capital gain upon the sale of the shares. The amount of the employee discount, or the difference between the price paid and the fair market value on

the date of purchase, will be included on your W-2 if you're a public company employee. When you sell the shares, the capital gain may be taxed at the lower long-term capital gain rate, depending upon how long you held the shares. A common mistake made after selling ESPP shares occurs when the sale is reported on your tax return: remember to add the employee discount amount that was included in your W-2 to the amount paid for the stock when calculating cost basis and gain.

> **Grant Date**—The date that an employee receives an equity award, such as stock options or restricted stock.

> **Vest Date**—The date the restrictions on stock options (generally based on time worked for a company) lapse, and the option to purchase stock no longer has a time- or performance-based restriction. Usually, vested shares are available for exercise and restricted stock becomes available for sale. However, specific company plans may allow for early exercise (subject to forfeiture if the shares are not vested), or may place additional restrictions on the stock. For example, a private company may not let restricted stock be sold until a change of control or an IPO.

> **Exercise Date**—The date when you elect to convert the options into actual shares of company stock by purchasing the shares at the predetermined price as set forth when granted.

> **Cashless Exercise**—An immediate sale of enough shares to pay the price of exercising the options, plus taxes, if applicable. Payroll, federal, and state taxes will usually be withheld, unless ISOs are exercised, in which case no withholding is taken.

> **Qualifying Dispositions (for ISOs)**—You must hold the stock two years from the date of the grant, and one year from the date of exercise. A qualifying disposition, where the stock is sold for more than the purchase price, is taxed favorably as a long-term capital gain.

> **Disqualifying Dispositions (for ISOs)**—If you fail to hold the stock for two years from grant date and one year from exercise date, the amount by which the fair market value on the date of exercise exceeds the strike price is treated as ordinary compensation income in the year

that you disposed of the stock. It should be included on the W-2 form you get from your company and the sale will not be subject to payroll taxes, such as FICA and Medicare. Special rules apply for stock sold at less than FMV at exercise and for exercise/sale transactions that straddle two tax years.

> **Restricted Stock Awards and Restricted Stock Units**—If you are granted restricted stock awards (RSAs) or restricted stock units (RSUs), there are no tax consequences at grant date. Upon vesting (or lapse of other restrictions), you receive shares of company stock. These shares are taxed at your ordinary income tax rate based on the value of the shares received. It's more common for larger companies than startups to issue RSUs or RSAs than stock options.

Your grant price (the value on the day you receive the restricted stock award) is irrelevant with this type of award. If you're not in a blackout period, you can sell the stock immediately upon receiving it. It acts like an ongoing bonus, as you stay with the company and vest, you receive a reward based on the current stock price. The day your stock vests, you receive taxable compensation based upon the fair market value of the shares, and your employer withholds taxes. The prudent move is usually to sell immediately; as you remain with the company, you'll continue to receive and vest in more shares.

> **Strike Price/Exercise Price**—This is the price paid when you exercise an option.

TIP 2   Early Exercise / 83(b) Election

As long as your company's plan allows it, you may exercise your options before they are vested. (The shares are still generally subject to vesting even though exercised.) By making a special election with the Internal Revenue Service, you can elect to pay tax on the bargain element at the early exercise date rather than later when you exercise the shares after they have vested. An 83(b) election is done to start the clock ticking for long-term capital gains. Special rules apply for ISOs, which should be considered before making an 83(b) election to early exercise. To get the favorable long-term capital gain tax rate applied to a gain on stock sales, you must hold the (exercised ISO) shares for at least two years from grant date and one year from exercise date. The early exercise of an ISO does not constitute an exercise for regular tax purposes, and the holding period for regular tax purposes does not start until the option would have otherwise vested. See the more comprehensive section on the pros and cons of early exercising your options on page 34.

TIP 3 Alternative Minimum Tax (AMT) Basics

The AMT is a tax system that runs parallel to the regular tax system for every United States taxpayer. Created in the 1980s, the goal of AMT is to limit the amount of tax deductions generally available to high-income tax-payers. There are two AMT tax rates: 26% and 28%. IRS Form 6251 calculates the AMT. When your tentative minimum tax exceeds your regular tax, you'll pay AMT tax (the excess of tentative minimum tax over regular tax). Exercising incentive stock options can trigger AMT, and it is just one of many types of adjustments to regular tax liability used to calculate AMT. Each U.S. taxpayer pays the higher of regular tax or AMT each year. In some situations, you can get an AMT credit to use to reduce your regular tax liability in a later year.[25] The AMT credit is a complex topic beyond the scope of this book.

TIP 4 Capital Gain

Capital gain occurs when a capital asset, such as stock or a mutual fund, is sold. Gain is the amount by which the sales proceeds exceed the asset's adjusted cost basis. Lower federal income tax rates are applied to long-term capital gains, defined as assets you've held for more than one year.

TIP 5 Stock Option Planning

Whether you have incentive stock options (ISOs) or non-qualified stock options (NQSOs), many tax planning strategies are available to you. Since there are many nuances to stock option planning, a complete under-standing and assessment of your specific circumstances should be undertaken, preferably with a tax professional, before you take any action with your options.

> **ISOs** require consideration of the following factors:

- Your marginal income tax rate on ordinary income versus the income tax rate on long-term capital gains. Generally, capital gains will be taxed at a lower rate than your ordinary income.

- The relationship between the exercise price of the option and the stock price on the day you exercise.

- Whether exercising ISOs will push you into AMT.

- The date you exercise (to determine when you must pay any taxes due).

- Whether you are required to make estimated tax payments.

- A realistic expectation for the price of the stock 12 months and one day after exercise. If the stock price is lower a year from the exercise date, it may make more sense to exercise and immediately sell the stock today and pay more tax than to hold on for a year hoping the stock price will go up. Examples abound (such as Groupon[26] and Zynga[27]) in which this buy-and-hold strategy did not work out for option holders who exercised but did not sell quickly, because the stock price dropped significantly after the IPO. Note that unless you are selling on the private market, you cannot sell company stock until Phase 3, after the company has gone public.

> **Non-qualified stock options** provide tax planning opportunities, too. Some of the important issues to consider are as follows:

- Whether you have the cash to exercise the options.

- Your investment portfolio diversification. (If you hold a lot of company stock, your concentrated position is a risky venture, although you may not be able to sell much, if any, stock until Phase 3.)

- Your cash flow needs.

- Whether you must make estimated tax payments.

- Nonfinancial factors, such as how long you plan to remain at the company and when you expect to retire.

- Your guess about the price of the stock at the end of 12 months and one day after exercise.

- Whether you have capital loss carryovers, which can be used to offset gain from stock sales dollar for dollar.
- In years of low income, exercising options is a way to generate additional taxable income to preserve itemized deductions that may otherwise be lost.

Before your liquidity event, consult with an accountant on the personal financial impact of taking action with equity awards. Multiyear tax planning includes pushing income to otherwise low-income years, taking deductions in high tax years, and/or using charitable planning strategies in conjunction with stock sales to reduce your taxes.

TIP 6   Planning with Restricted Stock

At the time your restricted stock vests, you'll owe tax on the full fair market value of the shares received. Restricted stock gets rid of the complexity and the exercise/hold scenario planning seen with stock options, because the shares at the time of vesting always have a basis equal to the fair market value on the day of vesting. Any further appreciation is taxed at either short- or long-term capital gain rates, depending upon how long you hold them. This sounds straightforward, yet there are several planning strategies to be mindful of.

> **Blackout Windows**—If you are subject to blackout windows because of your position in a publicly traded company, you can set up a 10b5-1 plan if your company allows it (see page 122).

> **Withholding Too Low**—One trap many people fall into is that their company withholds tax on restricted stock at a rate too low for an employee's tax bracket. The solution is to increase the withholding rate or make quarterly estimated tax payments.

> **Selling Shares to Pay Withholding Tax**—Some companies mandate selling a portion of your newly vested restricted stock unit (RSU) or restricted stock award (RSA) shares to pay for the withholding tax. If you don't like this idea, and you're bullish on the stock, buy shares of your company stock on the open market—although if your exposure to

the stock is more than 5% to 10% of your net worth, I wouldn't advise it.

> **Holding Stock**—Should you hold the vested restricted stock? You're taking on a lot of risk if you hold more than 10% of your net worth in the stock of any single company.

With restricted stock, says an experienced executive at Silicon Valley companies, "there's less of a psychological tug to ride out the upside, since the shares were purchased for the then fair market value."[28] Other factors to consider include the following:

- How many shares of restricted stock units (RSUs) or awards (RSAs) do you have?
- What is the vesting schedule?
- What percentage of your net worth is composed of the awards (and shares of stock in your company)?
- What's the current stock price?
- You're never underwater on the day you vest. But if you hold the restricted stock, and "if the company's doing really badly, they might not be worth all that much," says the executive, who during his career has been awarded both stock options and restricted stock units, and prefers RSUs.

TIP 7 Section 83(b) Election to Early Exercise Options

Some companies offer equity compensation through stock grants. For early employees, using the 83(b) election can start the clock on long-term capital gains (see page 31). It's best to make an 83(b) election on stock options when the spread between the exercise price and the fair market value is low. To understand what a Section 83(b) election is and how and when you might use it, it's a good idea to familiarize yourself with a few key terms.

When you have equity awards subject to forfeiture, they will usually be on a vesting schedule. Know when your shares *vest* and strategize when to *exercise* them. When your equity awards vest, you have the right to exercise them. A common vesting schedule is 25% of your options vest every year for four years. When your options vest, think about when you want to exercise them. *Exercise* means that you actually purchase the stock at the grant price or strike price.

Stock options and stock are not the same thing. Stock options give you the right to buy shares at a pre-determined price. For example, the company might give you the option to buy 10,000 shares for $0.50 per share. Later, the fair market value may be $10 per share. You don't actually have any ownership in the company—those 10,000 shares—until you exercise the options and buy the stock at the grant price or strike price. (If your strike price is $.50, you pay 50 cents per share to exercise the options.)

Generally, with non-qualified stock options you don't report any income until the exercise date, at which time you pay tax (at your ordinary income tax rate) on the difference between what you paid for the stock and the fair market value on the date of exercise. If the fair market value is much higher when the options vest than when you were granted them, you could be looking at a large tax payment as a result of exercising shares. (The rules for incentive stock options are slightly different: upon exercise, you may pay AMT, but not ordinary income; upon the sale, you may be able to use the AMT credit to offset regular income.)

A Section 83(b) election allows you to exercise early (before your options vest, usually while the stock price is still relatively low) to reduce the amount of taxes you have to pay. This way, you can presumably reduce the spread between your purchase price and the fair market value of the stock on the day you buy it. If you decide to participate in an 83(b) election, then you must file a statement with the IRS no later than 30 days after the date the property was transferred.[29] According to Kaye A. Thomas, author of *Consider Your Options*, failing to meet that 30-day deadline is the biggest problem with the Section 83(b) election. Thomas warns, "If you don't act within that time, you're out of luck. You can't wait until you file your return"[30] to make this election. "You have to do it right away."

Most advisors agree that if you think your company's stock price will increase, and your exercise price is low, you should consider exercising early because of the relatively low upfront cost and long-run tax benefits. Making an 83(b) election is a risky move, since the stock price could go down while you hold on to the shares. And, if you later forfeit the stock (voluntarily or not) after making the election, you cannot claim a deduction.[31]

> **Examples of the Section 83(b) Election**

Consider the following scenario:

- Say you were given a non-qualified option to buy 50,000 shares at $0.30 per share soon after a company started, and you are very optimistic about its future. The stock price is currently valued at $2 and there is talk that it will increase to $7 if your upcoming financing round goes well. If the company can successfully IPO in two years as planned, then, colleagues are telling you, the price might increase to $25 per share. If you sell all your shares at $25 per share, you would have a profit of $1,235,000 before taxes!

- The difference between the exercise price and the fair market value on the date of exercise is considered compensation income, taxable at your ordinary income tax rate. Any subsequent appreciation of the stock between when you purchased it and when you sell it is taxed at the more favorable capital gain tax rates, as long as you've held the shares for at least one year. A long-term capital gain rate of 20% is used in the examples that follow. (Note, though, that as of this writing, the federal long-term capital gain tax rate is 23.8% for those in the highest tax bracket.)

>> **Example A: No Early Exercise, Sell Stock at $25 per Share**

If you exercise your options when the fair market value is $25, the difference between the exercise price and the grant price ($25 – $0.30) gives you $24.70 per share of compensation income. This is "ordinary" income, taxed at your marginal tax bracket. If you're in the 40% tax bracket, your tax liability on the transaction would be $494,000. If you were to wait a year and a day from your exercise before selling, you could qualify for the long-term capital gain rate—the "promised land," as one interviewee called it—on the appreciation beyond what you purchased the stock for and what you sold it for. (Bear in mind that waiting another year after the IPO or liquidity event is always risky.)

Exercise Price = $15,000 ($0.30 x 50,000 shares)

Tax on Exercise = $494,000
($25 – $0.30 = $24.70 x 50,000 shares = $1,235,000 x 40%)

Sales Price (on day of exercise) = $1,250,000 ($25 x 50,000 shares)

Net After-Tax Proceeds from Sale = $741,000
($1,250,000 – $15,000 – $494,000)

Note: There's no tax on the sales price, because the sales price is equal to the fair market value on the date of exercise.

>> **Example B: Early Exercise via 83(b) Election, Sell at $25 per Share**

Contrast Example A with an early exercise via an 83(b) election. You purchase the shares for $0.30 each, when the market value is $0.30. The spread between the price you paid and the market value is $0 per share on 50,000 shares, meaning no appreciation is taxed as compensation income. The example below assumes you are in the 40% ordinary income tax bracket.

- If the share price rises as expected, any future gain beyond the exercise price of $0.30 per share is taxed at the lower capital gain tax rate, assuming you hold for at least one year. (The equation gets trickier if you're in a high tax bracket when you exercise and a lower tax bracket when you sell. Note that you may also be taxed if there's been appreciation in the stock between the grant date and the exercise date. A multiyear tax projection would be very helpful.)

Exercise Price = $15,000 ($0.30 x 50,000 shares)

Tax on Exercise = $0

Sales Price (two years after exercise) = $1,250,000

($25 x 50,000 shares)

Tax on Sale = $247,000

($25 – $0.30 = $24.70 x 50,000 shares = $1,235,000 x 20%)

Net After-Tax Proceeds from Sale = $988,000

($1,250,000 – $15,000 – $247,000)

In the above examples, the increase in after-tax sales proceeds from an early exercise would be $247,000. As you can see, with a smaller spread between exercise price and market value on the date of exercise, your risk from an early exercise is smaller, since you are paying less tax on the exercise.

> **Risks of an 83(b) Election**

In interviews with people who lived through the dot-com era, I heard over and over about tech employees who didn't take advantage of low-priced stock through an 83(b) election. Describing the late-'90s tech boom, this quote by a C-level executive echoes many: "One executive who didn't exercise his options early [he did not file an 83(b) election], exercised them after the company went public. He then had tax issues, and the stock went way down. He took a loan out to exercise the stock as well, to pay for the taxes, and the stock went way, way down. So he had the worst of all worlds: high taxes, and he couldn't sell his stock. It was as dumb as all get-out. [This was] an executive at a major, major company that rode the wave up, and then rode the wave down."[32]

In the examples above, I assumed that the stock's value was increasing, which is what created the tax savings. If the company's stock price drops after you exercise, then it's possible that you will end up paying too much tax.

Jason Graham, a CPA and tax advisor, told of some pre-IPO clients who got caught in this trap. For example, he consulted with a pre-IPO company whose internal valuation lost almost half of its value by the time it went IPO.[33] "Based upon how other similar companies have fared post-IPO, a number of the individuals at this company felt quite confident that a post-IPO price per share has got to be higher," Graham explained. "So they're thinking, it could be 1.5X, it could be 2X, it could be 3X. They were very bullish about where the company was going to go. And they had reasons for feeling that way. They felt like they kind of had a corner on that particular market that they've developed, they had a name for themselves, they had one successful venture after another, and that would continue."[34]

So some, filled with optimism about the company's future, exercised at a "healthy" price per share with a very low strike price and faced a significant tax bill with the hope that the fair market value would increase after the IPO. Graham encourages his clients working at startups to think about the downside possibilities of their action (or inaction) with stock options.

When it came time to determine what they could afford to exercise, some of the employees decided they would cover the taxes by selling their shares. The S-1[35] had been filed, so they assumed there would be enough time for the company to go public and their six-month lockup period to end before tax season. "I knew it was going to be a little tight," Graham remembers, "because I remember having conversations with them saying, 'You're going to need cash by April 15. So the hope was we can go public before October 15, so the six-month lockup comes off before April 15.' Well, that didn't happen. They were hoping it would, but I remember some delay in the IPO due to market volatility and timing, but then eventually it went public toward the end of the year."

Those employees managed to "scrape and borrow to get the taxes paid," but that was not the end of their troubles. "I would never have anticipated [the stock price] being so volatile so fast. You think about, in exactly one year's time, the stock dropped in value by 40% from its pre-IPO internal valuation to its opening price at IPO, while it was public it went up 40% from the opening price, but now [in mid-2012, it] is trading at less than 20% of its internal pre-IPO valuation, all within one year. That's a lot of up and down, a lot of volatility in one year," recalls Graham. "There's no predictability to it, there's no rhyme or reason to it." After our 2012 interview, the stock price fell even further. According to Graham, at that time most of the employees held their stock when it was trading at lower values, hoping it would recover to justify the high taxes incurred from the exercise.

This situation also brings to light another issue involved with participating in a Section 83(b) election: how to afford the upfront cost to exercise. Graham recommends his clients who are bullish on the stock borrow the cash to pay the taxes, insisting that "if they can do an early exercise, exercise all of [their options]." A tax payment on the spread when the stock price is low could make a substantial difference in the net sales proceeds later on. Many, he says, turn to family and friends for the cash. Before Oracle went public in 1986, CFO Roy Bukstein borrowed $4,000 from his dad to buy his pre-IPO shares. He encourages others who believe in the future of their company to borrow money to early exercise stock options.

Other pitfalls include the opportunity cost of paying the tax earlier rather than later and the restrictions placed on the options (such as losing the options if you leave the company). If you are new to options, then it is best to discuss your situation with a tax advisor before making a decision to participate in a Section 83(b) election. The rules for making the election are very specific, including the requirement of filing the election with the IRS and with your company within 30 days.[36]

> **How to Make the 83(b) Election**

Here are the requirements for an individual making an 83(b) election to early exercise equity awards:

1. Send a copy of the election to the IRS within 30 days of receiving the property (stock or options).
2. Provide a copy of the election to your employer.

❸ Attach a copy of the election to your tax return for the year the election is made.

❹ On your tax return, include the fair market value of the property received (less any amount paid for it) as compensation income; your employer should have added the amount to your W-2.

Taxpayers who receive stock with restrictions through the exercise of ISOs may be able to eliminate the AMT consequences by making an 83(b) election. The election in the case of ISOs simply increases the amount recognized for AMT purposes, allowing taxpayers to lock in the AMT consequences rather than waiting until the stock is vested.[37]

To protect yourself and avoid unnecessary correspondence with the Internal Revenue Service, it's best to follow these five steps:

❶ Complete the Section 83(b) election form provided by your employer. If you are married, have your spouse sign the election, too.

❷ Prepare a cover letter to the Internal Revenue Service (IRS).

❸ Send the cover letter with the originally executed Section 83(b) election form along with one copy of the form and a self-addressed stamped envelope so that the IRS may return a date-stamped copy of the Section 83(b) election to you.

❹ Mail the materials via certified mail, return receipt requested, to the Internal Revenue Service at the IRS address where you file your personal income tax returns. Have the package date-stamped at the post office, and retain the certified receipt that includes a dated postmark.

❺ Retain the IRS file-stamped copy along with the mail confirmations from the post office for your records for four years after the shares that the 83(b) election relates to are sold.

Checklist for Startup Employees in Phase 1

Review the items below during Phase 1 to optimize your personal financial wealth.

FOR EVERYONE WORKING IN THE STARTUP:

❏ Prepare an inventory of your stock, options, and other equity awards. Include the vesting schedule for each award. Understanding how your equity awards work will help you maximize your wealth.

❏ If your company allows it, consider making an 83(b) election on unvested stock options or restricted stock. If the cost to exercise your options and the "spread" are low, determine how much cash you'll need for both the exercise and the tax bill.

❏ If you are early exercising stock options, consider hiring an accountant for personal tax and cash flow planning.

❏ If you're taking a below-market salary, prepare a personal cash flow projection for at least two to three years to understand the commitment you will make to the startup.

❏ Try to objectively assess the potential for startup success, and if you see red flags for failure, consider whether to leave.

FOR EXECUTIVES:

❏ Hire an attorney who specializes in emerging growth companies to review your employment contract. Fight for your rights for a 100% double trigger (if not a single trigger).

❏ If you haven't already, put in place the ability for employees to make an 83(b) election to early exercise stock.

Phase 1 can last anywhere from two to 40 years. If your company has stalled in this phase, your personal finances can't support your needs, and funding options don't seem to be fast approaching, consider changing the course of your career here. Otherwise, continue on to Phase 2.

PHASE 2
RAMPING UP

Pre-Transition Phase
0–24 Months

The Four Phases of Startup Life[SM]

Phase 1	Phase 2	Liquidity Event	Phase 3	Phase 4
Pre-Transition 2-40 years **Laying the Foundation**	**Pre-Transition** 0-24 months **Ramping Up**		**Post-Transition** 1-24 months **Realizing the Dream**	**Into the Future** 2-40 years **What's Next?**

Quality of Life Challenges

Phase 1	Phase 2	Phase 3	Phase 4
Preoccupation with startup Loneliness Optimism Tenacity	Maintaining balance while working long hours Excitement Persistence	Weighing career options If you stay: Vest in peace and maintain work-life balance If you leave: Figure out what's next	Flexibility and choices Charitable activities Travel New career or startup Passion projects

Financial Challenges

Phase 1	Phase 2	Phase 3	Phase 4
Raising capital Below-market salary Accountability to investors Funnel all resources to create and build the company	Increasing enterprise value Salary and bonus Accountability to investors, management, and board Planning with equity awards	Increasing enterprise value and stock price Accountability to shareholders, board, and management Diversification of concentrated position Expensive purchases	New or second home Venture or angel investing Strategizing goals with financial resources

Common to All Phases

Challenge	Maximize Value of Equity Awards (ISO, NQ, RSA, RSU, ESPP)
Concerns	Wealth Preservation Tax Reduction Wealth Protection Passing Assets to Heirs Charitable Giving
Solutions	Personal CFO Expert Team of Advisors Financial Education

RAMPING UP

IT'S ALL ABOUT PERSEVERENCE in Phase 1, as you stay optimistic about your ideas and help to build the company. Because solving problems is a different skill set than creating a product,[1] be prepared to face new challenges in Phase 2 as your company prepares for a liquidity event. For example, the VCs might replace your CEO with someone more experienced, who may, according to Peter Herz, be "playing [more] for the VC firm, because that's where they're going to get their next gig," than for the best interest of the company. This is problematic for an unsuspecting startup. Or, as in the sad story of the creators of Dragon speech recognition software (see page 60), having investment bankers whose incentives clash with yours could cause you to lose both your company and your wealth.

In order to protect yourself as you ramp up toward your event, do your due diligence (i.e., kick-the-tires-type research) on executives introduced by your VC, attorneys, and investment bankers; prepare for surprises in the final moments before the deal; address your tax and financial situation with trustworthy accountants and/or financial planners before the deal is inked; and understand your equity awards and consider exercising.

All of this must be done in the midst of the super-stressful time at the tail end of Phase 2, when your company is trying to get the deal done—whether it's selling the company or filing for an IPO. In the final months of Phase 2, generally all employees and founders stay in place.

ROB NAIL'S JOURNEY TO A LIQUIDITY EVENT

CO-FOUNDER OF VELOCITY11, SOLD TO AGILENT IN 2007 FOR MORE THAN $100 MILLION.[2] ASSOCIATE FOUNDER, SINGULARITY UNIVERSITY.

Rob Nail is a salt-of-the-earth, humble, and curious guy. He is passionate about having a positive impact on humanity, creating cool technology, and being intellectually challenged,[3] and made his name as a founder and CEO of Velocity11, one of *Inc.* magazine's "Fastest Growing Companies of 2004." The company developed new technologies that changed the way scientists could conduct medical research and work on cures for diseases. After several failed attempts at being acquired, Velocity11 was bought by Agilent Technologies in December 2007. Nail's journey illustrates exactly how frustrating Phase 2 can be.

Nose to the Grindstone

As is true of most startups, the path was difficult from the outset. Nail believed in his company and gave up a lot of freedoms in his 20s to build it: "I was 100% focused on that. Relationships and other things, those did not exist. All I did was build the business." In order to invest more in the company's growth, the founders didn't pay themselves for the first 18 to 20 months. At the same time, they cashed in their stock from their previous company (missing a chance to triple their returns when that stock later shot up in value) and used the proceeds as working capital for Velocity11.

Although Nail and his co-founders had no income and growing personal debt, they pushed on. "At that point I think I had $70,000 on credit cards. I had personal loans out to friends and family, and the four of us were basically really starting to fight a lot. And we were making money. We had lots of revenue coming in, but everything we did was turning it back to 'How do we keep growing the business?'" Nail continues, "We were literally living in the office. And we tried to keep it a secret, but everybody knew, which is kind of funny. I had been living in my car and under the desk for a while."

The Lifeline

In 2001, two years after launching, another company offered Velocity11 a $20 million merger deal, which, considering the state of their personal finances, looked like the lifeline they needed. So they brought in an advisor. "One of the things he helped us realize was, if we each made $1 million, $1 million does not change the course of your life at all. You can't even buy a house around here for $1 million. If you get to the point where you made $10 million, that fundamentally will change your future in some interesting ways."

Nail and his team realized their company was worth more than they were being offered. Nail told the potential acquirer, "We really want to work with you. We think combined it could be amazing, but the balance is way off." At that point the Velocity11 management took a step that Nail describes as a nightmare. With an offer on the table, "we walked away from the deal." Not only were the founders "in an intensely needy point in [their] personal lives," but they had also prematurely basked in the company's merger with their employees. He remembers how "emotionally draining and horrible it was for everybody, and how long—it probably took six months—for everybody to get back into sync and feel like we're on track."

Emotionally exhausted and frustrated, Nail took off. He went to Nepal, climbed up Everest, and caught up on the life he thought he was missing. "And I realized how amazing what we were doing [at Velocity11] was, and how much I loved the group I was working with, and I have so much energy left. I was just burnt out at the time, so it was reinvigorating to realize I wasn't missing that much. I could go out anytime to go visit these places and do other stuff, but we have this great little family that we're building and we're doing some great work. So let's get back to it."

Attracting Investors

Soon after, they scored a major new customer and started paying the founders $30,000 a year. This let the founding team pay the minimum balance on their credit cards and, in Nail's words, "allowed us to live."

Their modest salaries increased to $80,000 after they went looking for investors. Nail laughs as he recalls the drastic shift in how investors reacted to Velocity11. "Any VC worth their salt in Silicon Valley in 2000, 2001 wouldn't touch anything that looked like a physical product. By 2002, 2003, we start talking to investors, and they're like, 'Wow, you have customers! You're profitable. You have huge growth.' We started to be very interesting." Incredibly, all of the eight VC groups he spoke to wanted to invest.

They teamed up with Mayfield, "and that created the next phase of the business," a phase which, to some extent, Nail says, "sucked. Over the next year, I hired five new executives, a whole VP layer; it was really disastrous, because it was a bunch of young kids. We grew this business—I think we probably had 50 to 60 people at the time— then we bring in this whole new executive layer on top of everybody, and it created this huge rift." What was tough for Nail was that he "had to bridge between those two constantly, though he admits it was ultimately necessary to have a management layer. "We didn't have the skill sets to continue to accelerate the growth."

In 2003 and 2004, Velocity11 explored a second offer, but it never got to the due diligence phase. Then, the management came across a compatible technology that, combined with Velocity11's hardware, could expand its market into the diagnostics field. They got everybody on board, went through due diligence, and were a week away from closing the deal. "At this point, we'd all been talking about buying cars, and buying a house, and we emotionally started investing our money elsewhere." This time, Nail decided not to tell the rest of the company. He was adamant about not dashing hopes. "We're not going to go through that again. We're going to manage expectations."

Unfortunately, his caution was warranted. "The COO of the acquiring company, who was going to be in charge of the integration and work with everything, quits and goes to another company." Its board decides it doesn't have "the ability to absorb this company now without that guy, so the deal's off. Literally, a week before it closed." Investment banks had money ready, integration strategies were in place, and legal documents were ready for signature. "It was nuts," sighs Nail. "That hurt." It's hard to put up complete emotional barriers a week before the deal is going to close.

Fourth Time's a Charm

After the third disappointment, the company spent four to five months getting the team back in order, cultivating sales and continued growth. "The business was never stronger. It was really doing well at that time." So Nail took an ultimatum to his board. Either he wanted to look into acquiring other technologies they identified, or "you let me go out and sell it. And we'll start another formal process, and we'll find a real partner, and we'll actually sell it." If they couldn't agree to either, then that was it for Nail. "My third plan was, I'm leaving and you can do whatever you want." After nearly eight years, he realized, "My 20s are gone, now my 30s are starting to rapidly flash by, and I don't know what we're going to do here. So they're like, 'OK. We'll start a real process.'"

They found an investment bank, pitched the companies, and stepped back and let the bank handle the negotiations. Before long, they had a deal with Agilent for the acquisition of Velocity11. Not only was this deal significantly larger than the one that fell through the year before, but also Nail was very optimistic about the future: "I was very emotionally excited about the potential to work at a big company as a general manager."

A provision of the deal put Nail in charge of integrating the two companies. He made sure that all of his employees still had a job after the acquisition and that Agilent respected Velocity11's workplace culture. Agilent even agreed to hang a key piece of company decor, a giant wind turbine propeller, which an employee brought into the Velocity11 office during its first year. "Every Friday we'd have happy hour, and new employees would get up on the scissor lift and sign the hub on the wind turbine. It became a company ritual."

Some changes didn't go as well. "We also had a dog policy, so [Agilent] had to allow us to bring dogs in, which was a big no-no anywhere else on the campus, which pissed everybody else off." But, ultimately, Nail was pleased with how things turned out. "I loved it. I thought, all these new people, all these new businesses, all these new products. I was excited about having my business there. I was very proud of it."

Personal Finances

His personal life post-liquidity, however, was less structured. Despite having full integration plans for the company, Nail had no plans for how to deal with his new wealth. Growing up and at college, "Nobody had money. I didn't need it. I didn't care about it. I didn't even know what I would do with it." For him, the company was never about the money.

After the Agilent acquisition, Nail relied heavily on his co-founders for advice on how to deal with his newfound wealth. Together, they decided to find a good financial advisor. The advisor "talked about the fully diversified portfolio, and investing and mixed strategies, all of which just didn't make any sense to me." While Nail is a brilliant engineer and understood the concept of diversifying, the many details around the fees were hard to follow, and he wanted assurances about performance in advance. "I want to invest in the ones that are going to make a bunch of money and not invest in ones that won't make any money, and I don't want to pay lots of fees."

He's not alone in this approach. Many engineers just want to handle their finances themselves and view the fees associated with financial planning as unnecessary and wasteful. The problem is, doing it yourself means you have to devote the time to making smart financial decisions as your personal situation and life change. You also need to watch the market and keep your emotions out of your decisions. "I tried to spend some amount of my free brain cells investigating investment strategies for different types of funds," Nail remembers. But finally he decided he'd rather focus on what he loved—his work—and outsource the financial piece. "I don't want to think about it. I'm trying to do this integration thing, so let's just plunk it down in someplace that I'm not going to lose all my money."

Risk and Maintain Buckets to Preserve Wealth

Nail didn't forfeit his ability to experiment with investing. He set aside an amount he could afford to lose (what I call the "Risk Bucket"), and self-managed these funds to learn about investing in companies he was passionate about, while the rest of his money—the part he could not afford to lose—was diversified with his financial advisor (the "Maintain Bucket"). "You're going to make some mistakes, and you have to find your feet in this new world. I probably paid more than I would have liked to on that front."

Part of his windfall went to giving back to the startup community through angel investing. "When I see another technology that I see has great potential, it makes total sense for me to want to invest in that, because that's what I've been doing for 10 years." He also has a few words of warning for others looking to angel invest. "Sometimes, what you see is not always what you get. I had a couple friends that I trusted who I didn't get the complete story from and lost [a ton of] money." His advice? "Spend more time really understanding the details of [the] business, actually doing more diligence than just trusting [a friend]."

Transitioning Out

Nail spent two years at Agilent before deciding the fit just wasn't right. After he left, he spent time investing, surfing, and just hanging out. He also got married. His current position as the CEO and Associate Founder of Singularity University, an institution that help students use technology to tackle some of the most pressing challenges of our times, is a perfect fit that just fell into his lap. Nail acknowledges his good fortune: "Wow, this is the community I was looking for. It really just extended everything I ever wanted to a global scale." He urges others in a similar situation to "just be open to the things, and if they line up with what you want to do in life, just kind of follow them and see where it goes."

■ ■ ■ ■

Holding the Deal Ransom

As Rob Nail's story illustrates, a deal can fall apart at any moment. So while Phase 2 is all about "transitioning to the liquidity event," one engineer and serial entrepreneur who requested privacy[4] says it's rarely an easy transition to make. "Every liquidity event that I've ever been involved in, there comes a moment where people have to buy off," and someone has to sacrifice for the greater good of the others. Issues can range from a particular clause in an employment contract or a developer's patent, to a transferability or share valuation issue for the buyout or conversion. Below are some examples of last-minute surprises seed investors and co-founders can bring up late in Phase 2—generally in the month before the liquidity event—that require tough conversations and intense last-minute negotiations.

- "The person in the company that has a change-of-control clause in their contract. And guess what? The deal's not going to get done if they keep their change of control.
- "The person whose stock might be underwater, but it's the right thing to do for the company to liquidate at that rate. But they're not going to vote for it, because their stock is underwater, so you've got to get them past that.
- "The early investor who feels that you should hold off on an acquisition [and instead go public at a later time].
- "The five employees that realize that their stock isn't going to be worth what they thought it was going to be worth, and they want to vote against [the liquidity event].
- "One of the early guys who was in the company decides that one of the patents that he had signed over to the corporation wasn't signed over properly. There was some sort of patent transfer that hadn't quite executed according to his lawyer. So he was going to say, 'You can't take the IP [intellectual property] unless you buy me off for XYZ price.' And that was literally at the 11th hour," as they were getting ready to sign documents to sell the company, remembers the engineer and entrepreneur. The team negotiated, and the employee probably got more than he deserved, but the deal went through.

While he claims to have mellowed with age, he is a natural peacemaker. Last-minute team negotiations sometimes come down to a straight-shooting conversation, acknowledging the team members' years of work for the company and the existing contract terms, while stressing the need for a personal sacrifice. Whether he's serving in the capacity of CEO or entrepreneur, his 11th-hour conversations go something like this: "We have two ways to do this. You can scuttle the whole deal, and everyone around here will basically not be rewarded. Or you can give up on this benefit for yourself, and for the greater good get this deal done. What do you want to do?"

For this engineer and entrepreneur, business success is all about the team. "Great teams can take average products and make huge markets out of them," he says. "And poor teams can take great products and destroy them. So if you can find the right team and you can find the right folks, then you can generally make the negotiations easier."

The lesson here: always expect surprises.

A DEALMAKER'S SPENDING ADVICE

Sylvia Yam has a unique perspective on mergers and acquisitions. She was an M&A analyst at JPMorgan in New York before moving to California to work on corporate development for Yahoo.[5] In three years at the Sunnyvale-based Internet pioneer, she closed about 10 deals, "ranging from $1 million to $4 billion," she remembers. "I'm a big believer in not spending before you're certain" about your wealth event, confides Yam. "There are no guarantees. A deal can fall apart the day before you think it will. . . . You can sign everything, and then decide to withhold the fund transfer if you find something in due diligence," she says, such as a lawsuit, from the acquirer's point of view. "There are no guarantees until the money's transferred."

Overspending, Leverage & Lost Opportunities

Since so many issues can derail a deal at the last minute, you want to make sure your company, your sanity, and your personal financial security survive if negotiations fall through. But how can you stay rational when you can practically taste your impending (paper) millions?

Finding happiness while living below your means is a key to preserving your wealth and contentment. In Phase 2, it's especially important not to overspend. Rob Nail, profiled on page 46, knew this. That's why as soon as the business would allow it, he paid himself and his executives a modest base salary so that they could pay down their credit cards.

There have been many spectacular flameouts in the high-tech community. The water coolers and watering holes of Silicon Valley are rife with tales of paper millionaires who didn't diversify, spent money based on their stock's value—not cash in the bank—and wound up with nothing.

For example, in the dot-com heyday, "people assumed their paper wealth was real wealth, and it's all concentrated in one stock." When Pets.com went public with an insane valuation, the founders and executives "on paper were worth gazillions of dollars," explains Marc Tarpenning. "They then borrowed against their shares and bought giant houses in Atherton and Burlingame, and [other] fancy neighborhoods, and then of course, by the time they could sell the shares, they were worth one hundredth or one thousandth of what they thought they were going to be worth, and ended up being foreclosed on, and having friends and family bailing them out."

This enthusiasm didn't just cloud the judgment of executives, says Tarpenning. "Regular employees did the same thing. They had these options, and they're suddenly worth tens of millions of dollars, and they didn't want to sell. They didn't want to exercise and take [their wealth off the table], because it's only going to go up. So they would instead borrow lots of money and build a giant house, and then of course they lost the house and everything."

At one time, Cisco was the most valuable company on earth, and a lot of employees had options, says Tarpenning. The employees felt they were infinitely wealthy. Then, of course, the stock dropped a bit, and it dropped below their strike price, so their paper wealth went to zero. Even if their underlying stock went to $60, the strike price was at $150, so it's a zero net result.

Overconfidence can be very dangerous. If you get lucky once, you should take at least some of your profits off the table.

Look Out for Yourself!

Although it's unpleasant to think about, your company may be shielding you from the information you need to make successful financial decisions and set yourself and your family up for the future. Some people in upper management believe employees should never plan for a possible liquidity event. Rather, they should keep their fingers on their keyboards 80 hours a week and create great products. If a liquidity event happens, then, these people believe, they should start planning.

A former chief operating executive at three Fortune 100 companies who has sat on many startup boards of directors shared this: "We used to go out of our way NOT to prepare employees for any liquidity because of the shareholders' desire to keep them focused on the company's mission, and also because of the uncertainties involved. Preparing employees in advance of an event, unless it is in one of the small handful of rare and very mature situations (such as Google or Facebook), is probably not in the company's interest prior to the event."[6]

Does this sound like a double standard? The executive who explained this to me currently works with five management teams and is compensated for his consulting work in two ways: a monthly fee, which is relatively low, and an equity component. "I've earned far more from the equity component than the monthly fees," he says. He's been planning for his future. So why shouldn't executives and employees be educated about how to do the same?

In a two-hour interview with this seasoned high-tech exec, he spoke excitedly about the changes he's seen over the decades. He even postponed his next appointment so that he could extend our interview. He loved talking about his experience and current consulting projects. About a week after our interview, I got an email from him reaffirming his stance on when companies should educate employees, which conflicts with my view in favor of early education.

"It is not in any company's interest to prematurely engage their employees in any post-liquidity financial wealth discussion," he wrote. "So from a shareholder's [and] company-building perspective, your Phases 1 and 2 are dysfunctional." Because of the uncertainty surrounding "when, how, and at what value eventual wealth may occur," he wrote, it's "better to advise all to wait until it actually happens, and to not spend any time on how to spend money they don't have. Often [their] 'wealth' is on paper; the timing and valuation of their asset is uncertain, or there is a timing lockup, or there is the uncertainty of a forward-looking earnout, so the individual is unable to create immediate liquid value." He concluded, "An entrepreneur, who in your Phase 3 actually receives liquid cash is not that different from any other individual who wins the lottery or inherits wealth. I suggest that you start your phases from after the person has experienced material cash, free and clear, from your Phase 3 or beyond."

I firmly disagree. Waiting until Phase 3 is too late to start planning for your financial future. Exercising low-priced stock options and creating a cash flow plan are two important actions to take in the early phases of a startup.

While I strongly advise that you put some thought and consideration into your personal financial plan before the liquidity event, you don't want to go overboard with enthusiasm. Attorney Jim Koshland, who helps form and advise technology companies, cautions against doing too much planning beforehand, since this time is "an unknown period," and it's questionable "whether there really is going to be value created."[7] While he doesn't advise on individual planning, he's seen enough to know the basics of smart financial planning with equity awards. "If you knew it was going to be very valuable, it would be a lot easier. You could do a lot of things, like gifting to kids [and other planning techniques], earlier on that make a lot of sense, but a lot of people don't do it, because one, they don't know [what the ultimate liquidity will be], and two, it's a little bit jinxing." Koshland, a thoughtful, direct man, doesn't mince words when he advises early employees and founders to buy "as much stock as cheaply and as early on as possible."

Koshland summarizes where both advisors agree: "For individuals, building a great company and not worrying about liquidity is the most important thing, because I think liquidity will happen. Don't worry, but take a few steps to plan for it."

Does your company or board of directors shield you from being educated about your own personal financial planning?

STAY FOCUSED AND KEEP SHIPPING

Mark Zuckerberg had the forethought to encourage employees to keep focused on their jobs rather than the stock price—or to "stay focused & keep shipping"[8]—leading up to and after Facebook's May 2012 IPO. The message had an impact. In the year after Facebook's IPO, the stock price dropped dramatically. Yet, most employees stuck around, and as of this writing in early 2014, the stock price has surpassed the IPO level.

Figure 1. Posted on Mark Zuckerberg's Facebook Wall, February 1, 2012, with the caption, "My desk—at Facebook HQ."[9]

Yelp's Max Levchin and His Roth IRA

The decisions you make—or fail to make—in Phases 1 and 2 can strongly impact how you emerge from a liquidity event. Read on for stories of how things can go right, and how they can go very, very wrong. While the success tales below come from very wealthy folks, these strategies can be implemented on a smaller scale if you have company stock with high-growth potential. A note of caution, however: if you make a big bet using retirement funds without sufficient assets apart from these funds, and that bet is wrong, you may risk a comfortable financial future.

Computer scientist turned angel investor Max Levchin has experienced many successes. He broke onto the technology scene as a co-founder and CTO of PayPal; in the year PayPal was sold to eBay, Levchin was later named "Innovator of the Year" by MIT's *Technology Review* magazine. Next, he founded Slide.com, which was acquired by Google for $200 million.[10] More recently, he has been serving as the chairman of the board of Yelp, an online consumer review service for businesses, and is compensated with equity. (The SEC Form S-1 registration dated 2010 lists Levchin owning more than 28 million shares and selling more than seven million prior to the IPO.)[11]

He made headlines again soon after Yelp's IPO, but not because of the amazing technology he had created. Instead, he and Facebook's Mark Zuckerberg and Dustin Moskovitz were profiled for their shrewd financial planning techniques in an article on Forbes.com, "How Facebook Billionaires Dodge Mega-Millions in Taxes."[12]

Levchin and the Facebook executives used different strategies, all with effective results. As a privileged early investor in Yelp, Levchin was able to purchase stock using cash in his Roth IRA account. What's so special about that? All earnings in a Roth IRA are tax-free, as long as Levchin waits until he is at least 59½ before taking the money out. (There are a few circumstances in which it's OK to take disbursements from a Roth IRA earlier, but they are rare.) And Levchin could avoid taking withdrawals for his entire life, even if he lives to be 100. That means that the 3.1 million shares he sold in his Roth IRA in the year of the IPO for a $10 million profit won't face any income taxes during Levchin's life or the life of his Roth IRA's heirs (if his grandchildren inherit the Roth IRA, this tax-free wealth could stretch out for a century or more, as long as the heirs live). In early 2012, SEC filings showed that Levchin still had 3.9 million shares in his Roth IRA post-IPO,[13] which will have the same favorable result.

CPA Jason Graham explains this technique in more detail. "You can't just transfer assets into a Roth IRA. A Roth IRA has to buy assets with cash. If you look at the S-1s for companies like Facebook and Yelp, you can see that ownership in the stock is sometimes held in Roth IRAs. With the cash some early investors had in their Roth IRAs, they used their Roth IRA account to buy the pre-IPO stock."[14] When the stock purchase happened, explains Graham, "the individual might not be on the board at the time. That's the other tricky thing with Roth IRAs. If an individual is on the board, it's possible they still may have been able to buy the shares in the Roth IRA, but with Roth IRAs, you have to be careful you don't run afoul of certain rules. For example, if you control or have ownership of more than 50% of the company, you can't buy shares in a Roth IRA, because it's viewed as you are benefiting yourself. And you can't, in any form or fashion, use a Roth IRA that would make it look like you were somehow benefiting yourself."

Graham brings up a situation in which someone might run afoul of the IRS and Department of Labor rules because of compensation issues. "If you, for example, have a Roth IRA and it has cash, and you have it buy into a company that you're working for, then—and it might be an extreme view—but the IRS could take the argument like, well, you're putting money into a company that's paying you a salary, so you're indirectly helping your salary, because you're helping the company get more money, and therefore the company has the ability to pay you a larger salary. That might be splitting hairs, and someone could probably defeat that argument, but those are the types of things that people have to think about."

How Facebook Founders Transferred Wealth

Four years before the Facebook IPO, co-founders Mark Zuckerberg and Dustin Moskovitz each set up grantor retained annuity trusts (GRATs). Just before the IPO, those GRATs were estimated by *Forbes* to transfer a total of at least $185 million gift tax-free to their non-charitable beneficiaries.[15] Read about the technical details of this strategy on page 67.

For the executive who has reached Phase 3 a few times and jumps back again and again to Phase 1 to create new companies, this type of estate planning can be an ideal way to minimize transfer taxes. But for those with only paper wealth, Graham advises, "It doesn't make sense to create any kind of complexities or structures when you don't even have anything yet." Instead, you want to use it when you hope the stock put into the GRAT "is going to grow into something. It's what I refer to as a freeze technique, in that you're freezing the value of where it is today. The appreciation is what you're giving away, and that could be substantial, because if you're dealing with a pre-IPO company that's going to go 3X, then you're going to be able to give away all that upside without incurring any transfer taxes." In the worst-case scenario, if your company goes bankrupt or the price takes a nosedive, you'll be out accounting and attorney fees. You can still get the stock back (even though it's worth much less).

Levchin, Zuckerberg, and Moskovitz had great personal financial advisors to guide them through Phases 1 and 2, a time when it's hard to step away from work to plan for your financial future. But not all advisor collaborations result in success.

Cautionary Tale: Dragon Systems

If you've seen the heartwarming ads on television in which a blogger speaks thoughts as they're automatically typed up, a teenage boy updates his Facebook status just by talking, and a poor typist, whose Italian immigrant parents couldn't write, can now speak and have her family's history autotyped, you probably think that the creators of Dragon voice recognition software must be wealthy geniuses. Well, you're half-right.

James and Janet Baker, founders of Dragon Systems, were not so lucky in their choice of advisors. Their story is especially sad, because not only did they lose their net worth in the company they spent decades building, but they also lost their software in an acquisition deal gone bad. And they were not done with their creation. Both PhDs and "credited with advancing speech technology far faster than anyone thought possible," they were involved in "the business deal from hell," according to the *New York Times.*[16]

Passionate about accomplishing elegant speech recognition, James Baker incorporated an algorithm based on the probability that one sound followed another, rather than trying to teach the computer how to interpret accents and dialects. Over many decades, the Bakers built and refined their software products to interpret voice commands. The Bakers considered taking Dragon public, but soon offers to acquire Dragon Systems started rolling in from companies like Sony and Intel.

At this point, the Bakers wanted guidance on how best to manage all the incoming offers and to perform due diligence on potential acquirers. At that time, "Goldman was the alpha dog in the lucrative game of mergers and acquisitions," and the Bakers hired the investment bank known for its "ruthless professionalism" for a $5 million flat fee.[17] Though Dragon was the culmination of their long careers' work and, according to the *Times*, a "third child" to the Bakers, it was small potatoes to Goldman Sachs, who assigned four bankers to the deal—ages 21, 25, 32, and 42—dubbed "The Goldman Four" later, when post-deal trouble began.

As talks with other companies stagnated, the *Times* story continues, a representative from Goldman accompanied Janet Baker and Dragon's CFO to Belgium to meet with the executives Lernout & Hauspie (L&H), who proposed a $580 million deal, half in cash, half in company stock. The Bakers weren't completely sold, as news had recently been circulating about L&H's questionable revenue growth in the Asian markets. The rumors turned out to be true.

While the Bakers were very concerned about L&H's stock price volatility, they believed, incorrectly, that Goldman's analysts had been covering L&H and would communicate any dangers to the Goldman Four team. It would have been easy for Goldman's analysts to call up the customers of L&H and check the numbers—which, unfortunately for the Bakers, their Goldman team didn't request, nor did the Goldman Four feel compelled to do themselves.

When it came time to make an agreement, no Goldman representatives attended the meeting; a few days beforehand, the *Times* reports, the Goldman contact said he would be away on vacation and couldn't make the meeting, nor would anyone else from Goldman attend. Further, the agreement was changed at that meeting from half stock to all stock. And without anyone from Goldman at the meeting to advise them, the Bakers inked the deal.

One month later, the story broke that L&H had been fabricating sales data. (All it took to crack the case? A few calls to customers L&H claimed to have, who denied all sales.) The stock and everything the Bakers had to show for their life's work were worthless. "The money was one thing. But what they really wanted was the opportunity to complete the work they had started decades earlier"[18] (the agreement also stipulated that the Bakers would work at L&H after the acquisition). On top of everything, they couldn't even get their technology back. It was sold at an auction after L&H went bankrupt.

It then surfaced that two years earlier, Goldman had looked closely at L&H. Goldman, itself, had considered investing $30 million in the company but backed out after preliminary due diligence, which included calling the customers.

During a deposition in the lawsuit brought by the Bakers against Goldman Sachs, the Goldman Four insisted they gave the Bakers "great advice." The Goldman Four were repeatedly asked to clarify how the advice had been so good when the Bakers lost everything. The Goldman bankers' response? "We guided them to a completed transaction."[19]

LESSONS LEARNED FROM THE DRAGON SYSTEMS TRAGEDY

Seasoned M&A attorney Marlee Myers understands that the investment bank had only one goal.[20] "Anybody who gets a fee at closing—only if the deal closes—is optimized for you to sell the company."[21] As for the due diligence the Bakers expected, "There are people at Goldman who know how to do it. They do it when they're making an investment or taking a company public, but due diligence is generally not in the job description when they are functioning as a sell-side investment banker.

"Perhaps if [the Bakers] had the kind of lawyer who really functioned as their business partner, they may have known better. I would advise any client not to rely on their investment bank for due diligence," cautions Myers.

Another question that the Bakers might have considered: When selling a company, is it appropriate to have an investment banker or business broker in addition to a lawyer and an accountant?

"Yes, often it's very appropriate," says Myers. "That's a question you ask yourself in every deal. 'Do we actually need an investment banker who's going to take a minimum fee that could be millions of dollars off the top?' In some deals you don't need one, but in others you really do.

"There are three major things that investment bankers can bring to the table," Myers continues. "One is price discovery. They can help you figure out what your business is worth." Second, if you get the right banker, they will "connect you to potential buyers. Also, if you are running an auction-type process, they can manage the process so that it is orderly and leads to the highest bid." Finally, i-bankers "can help to negotiate the price and terms" of the deal.

Although the Bakers did seek outside help—the "best," or so they thought— it seems that they were missing a legal champion and a consultant or advisor who specialized in business and financial due diligence. What they didn't understand are the limits on what investment bankers do and the adverse motivations between client and investment banker. "Basically, an investment banker can be very helpful if you understand that what they are optimized for is getting the deal done," Myers explains. Someone who gets a large minimum fee for closing the deal, regardless of your net proceeds or goals, has little incentive to advise you to walk away. If your advisor (or banker, lawyer, or financial planner, for that matter) lacks incentive to act on your behalf, you could experience unpleasant surprises and disappointment.

A better idea in these situations is to hire a team of advisors who are working to optimize your success. For legal help, "you really need to find someone that you click with and is excellent at what they do—at the lawyer things, but also just really understands what your objectives are and how to achieve them. That's their job." Likewise, she suggests complementing legal advice with a corporate accountant or "a due diligence consultant who is going to ask a lot of hard questions about the numbers and is going to do some digging if, like the Bakers, you are being paid in stock rather than cash." Via email, Myers explains: "Diligence on the buyer should have been extremely important to them. They shouldn't have assumed that Goldman would do the diligence for them; this is not typically the i-banker's job." Additionally, "a seller who is being paid in stock of the buyer should not rely on their investment banker for financial and business diligence on the buyer. Of course, in a cash deal, that type of diligence isn't needed."

Think carefully about the advisors you choose. Investment bankers have their own skill sets, and their motivation can simply be to close the deal rather than see you achieve your goals—whether you desire more money or a specific next step in your career (in the case of a merger or acquisition). It's a good idea to have unbiased attorneys and accountants on your team whose incentives are allied with yours. For more information about including investment bankers in your deal, see my book *Startup Wealth*.

Consequences of Staying in Phase 2 Longer than Expected

Not all startups get to a liquidity event. "There is somewhat of a lottery culture," says one VC, and "there are some great people who don't make money."[22]

Brendan Richardson, Professor of Entrepreneurship and Venture Capital Investing at the University of Virginia's McIntire School of Commerce, speaks from real-world experience. While the founders and the management team are being paid a salary, they may live modestly until the startup gets "some traction."[23] When a lucky one reaches Phase 2, he says, "The company is successful and growing fast. You're focused on value creation. You're focused on creating harmony while working long hours, because you've found that business model that scales. The flywheel is spinning, and you are off to some exit. It's just unclear how big or where that exit is going to be."

However, Richardson cautions, "Most startups don't ever get to that phase. They don't ever find the thing that begins to scale. And oftentimes, they pivot one or more times trying to find that scalable model. So you can bounce around in Phase 1 for many, many years, and through many, many pivots in many, many startups as an individual."

Personally, "I'm still in Phase 1, still chasing the dream," admits Richardson, who is warm, intelligent, and insightful. He's worked in a variety of roles as a venture capitalist in the startup world for two decades. "I'm still in Phase 1, meaning my net worth is not at a point where I don't think about work anymore. So I'm still working for a salary. I'm still doing things that pay me on a regular basis, as opposed to creating enough wealth that I just pay myself to do what I want to do."

Richardson has seen multiple deals fall through at the very last minute. "I have seen, sadly, a number of times, what appears to be a liquidity event on the horizon, and it doesn't happen. Something occurs in the market, something occurs personally, or for some reason or another that liquidity event doesn't materialize." Sometimes, in Richardson's view, "the management team focuses so much on the liquidity event, they've sort of stopped managing the business." So when the event doesn't happen, the business is in tatters, as well. "It's like the wheels come off the train and they never get to the liquidity event, and they end up shutting the company down," he says.

Richardson gives an example of a French company in his VC portfolio that created backup and restoration software for large companies and partnered with Microsoft for distribution. Richardson recalls: "Microsoft made an investment, and the belief was that Microsoft was going to buy them." Microsoft kept saying, according to Richardson, "'This is great. Can you just do this for us so it works better with .net architecture? What we really love about this product is this, not so much this. Why don't you guys focus on that part that we love?'" Because Microsoft was a partner and investor, the management team had the feeling that "'Wow, this is the woman we're going to marry.' And then, it turned out Microsoft came out with their own version of this [software]. And we went from being the one and only, we're dating exclusively, to 'You know what? I've been seeing other people and I got a better offer over here, so I'm not really interested in dating anymore. And not only am I not interested in dating, but we certainly don't want to get married.'"

The Microsoft partnership had been going on for years, so this company had redirected its entire architecture to work with Microsoft and ignored all the other players in the market. In Richardson's words, "They were left, not quite at the altar, but they had moved, they had sold the house, they had done everything to be with this partner, and the partner decided, 'no thanks.'" As for the company? The investors lost focus. The management team lost focus. "The whole thing basically came to a grinding halt. The management team was buying homes based on this outcome that they thought was going to happen, and the investors were excited and putting money into it based on what they thought was going to happen. And then it literally, over the course of about a month, all completely reversed direction."

The bottom line is to keep running your business and focus on your products and customers as if that liquidity event is not going to happen. "Even though the liquidity event may look like a 98% certainty," Richardson cautions, "it's actually much lower than it appears. Therefore, you want to make sure that if a meteor strikes the earth the day before your liquidity event closes, you still have a business to run the day after. Because all sorts of stuff can happen.

"It wasn't in our portfolio," Richardson continues, "but I know companies that were set to close on acquisitions, on both sides of the table, and the closing was set to happen on September 14, 2001." In that case, "Everything is off the table." Richardson acknowledges this is an extreme example, but cautions people not to consider the deal done before it's done: "If you're banking on that liquidity event to happen, and 9/11 comes along or something equally disruptive in your particular market—and it could literally be the manager from the acquiring company who's running the deal breaks his ankle and is in the hospital for surgery for the next two months—and the deal basically loses momentum and unravels."

Running out of cash is also a concern about hanging out in Phase 2 for too long. "I can't tell you how many companies I've worked with have great ideas, good traction, just about there, and they ran out of money. It's just a shame," says well-known and respected Silicon Valley transactional attorney Mark Cameron White.[24]

YOUR HAPPINESS AND FINANCIAL FUTURE

If you're not on track for a liquidity event at your current company and you're unhappy about it, reassess your life plan, and figure out if you should make a job or career change to achieve your goals. Feeling dissatisfaction with the direction of the company—especially if you've been working too long with a below-market salary and no benefits—can happen. Understand that you may not physically be able to work forever. Thus, if you're not independently wealthy, it's a good idea to look at your assets and goals and determine your next move.

Do you have the resources to continue in your standard of living? Do you have the flexibility of stopping work at some point in the future?

In the event that you need to stop working at age 65 or 75, are you on track with your savings? Will you have earned enough to accomplish your goals? I suggest hiring a professional financial planner to help you get a clear picture of what you've accumulated, what you spend, your future expenses (such as college education or a new home), and to create an action plan. Refer to my BE WISE Planning Strategy™ in the appendix for a comprehensive guide to help you strategize how to spend your time and your money when you decide to stop working.

FINANCIAL PLANNING AND TAX TIPS

TIP 8 A Wealth Transfer Strategy: GRATs

GRATs, or grantor retained annuity trusts, are a wealth transfer strategy that freezes the value of estate assets and allows people to transfer appreciation of property to children or other beneficiaries gift and estate tax-free.[25] "They are also a way to leverage the estate and gift tax exemption," says San Francisco estate planning attorney Beth L. Kramer. GRATs operate as follows: the grantor (the person setting up the GRAT) contributes shares of stock or other property to an irrevocable trust and reserves the right to receive an annual payment from the trust over a stipulated period of time. If the grantor survives that period, then any assets left in the trust will be passed to his or her specified beneficiaries or to a trust for their benefit. (If the grantor does not survive the term, some or all of the GRAT will be included in the taxable estate of the grantor.) The grantor has some flexibility to direct how the remainder beneficiaries receive the remainder interest at the end of the GRAT term.

When the GRAT is established, the grantor reports a gift of the remainder interest of the GRAT based on the value of the gift at that time, less the value of the lifetime annuity interest (the present interest of the total of the annual payments). The annuity interest is valued using IRS-specified interest rates. GRATs can be structured so that the annuity interest equals the value of the assets contributed so that the remainder interest is valued at zero. For all GRATS, if the **assets** grow at a rate equal to or less than the IRS-specified interest rate, then the grantor will receive payments large enough so that nothing is left for any beneficiaries. If the assets grow at a greater rate than the IRS-specified interest rate, then the excess is passed to the remainder beneficiaries without being subject to gift tax. Ultimately, assuming the GRAT assets appreciate at a rate greater than the IRS-specified rate, GRATs allow the grantor to transfer wealth in excess of the exemption amount, because there is no gift tax on the appreciation of GRAT property.

TIP 9   Alternative Minimum Tax (AMT) Triggers

The alternative minimum tax is a parallel tax system running alongside the regular federal income tax. When your AMT is higher than your regular tax, you'll pay AMT. The top AMT tax rate is 28%.

The most common items that cause individuals to fall into AMT are state taxes, property taxes, and the exercise of incentive stock options (ISOs). State and property taxes are allowed as a deduction from your regular tax but not for AMT, so they effectively increase your AMT tax. When you exercise and hold ISOs, the bargain element—the difference between your option strike price and the fair market value on the date you exercise them—is added to your AMT income.

Tax planning at the end of the year is helpful to analyze your situation and recommend an appropriate plan.

> **If you are not in AMT,** and anticipate a large state tax bill for the year, you'll get a federal tax deduction by paying your state tax by December 31. This planning tool is most useful for people in high-tax states such as California and New York. Alternatively, if you have unexercised ISOs, you can exercise and hold them and pay no tax on the transaction, as long as your AMT doesn't exceed your regular tax. The advantage of exercising and holding ISOs is that you'll get the long-term capital gain holding period started.

> **If you are in AMT,** some typical tax deductions will have the opposite effect; they will not decrease your tax liability. If you are in AMT already—for example, perhaps you've paid a large amount of state taxes, claimed many personal exemptions, or have exercised ISOs—you will not want to pre-pay state taxes or property tax. If you expect an additional state tax liability for the current year, make any fourth quarter estimated tax payment in January of the following year.

Checklist for Startup Employees in Phase 2

Review the items below when you are in Phase 2 to optimize your business success and personal wealth.

FOR EVERYONE WORKING IN THE STARTUP:

❏ Stay focused on building the enterprise's value, because a successful liquidity event is not guaranteed.

❏ Prepare for last-minute surprises before the acquisition, merger, or IPO is finalized, and don't spend your paper wealth until you have cash in hand.

❏ Prepare an inventory of your stock, options, and other equity awards. Include the vesting schedule for each award. Understanding how they work will help you maximize your wealth.

❏ If you can make an 83(b) election with little out-of-pocket cost, do so. Remember to submit an election form to both your company and the IRS, and also attach it to your tax return for the tax year in which you made the election (see pages 34 to 41).

❏ If you are early exercising stock options, consider hiring an accountant for personal tax and cash flow planning. If you already have assets, a financial planner with tax expertise can help you understand your cash flow and financial picture before and after your wealth event.

FOR EXECUTIVES:

❏ Hire an attorney who specializes in executive compensation issues for startups to represent your personal interests before you sign contracts, if you have the opportunity to renegotiate before the event.

❏ Do your due diligence on attorneys and tax advisors before hiring.

LIQUIDITY EVENT

THE PAYOFF

The Four Phases of Startup Life[SM]

Phase 1	Phase 2	Liquidity Event	Phase 3	Phase 4
Pre-Transition 2-40 years **Laying the Foundation**	**Pre-Transition** 0-24 months **Ramping Up**		**Post-Transition** 1-24 months **Realizing the Dream**	**Into the Future** 2-40 years **What's Next?**

Quality of Life Challenges

Phase 1	Phase 2		Phase 3	Phase 4
Preoccupation with startup Loneliness Optimism Tenacity	Maintaining balance while working long hours Excitement Persistence		Weighing career options If you stay: Vest in peace and maintain work-life balance If you leave: Figure out what's next	Flexibility and choices Charitable activities Travel New career or startup Passion projects

Financial Challenges

Phase 1	Phase 2		Phase 3	Phase 4
Raising capital Below-market salary Accountability to investors Funnel all resources to create and build the company	Increasing enterprise value Salary and bonus Accountability to investors, management, and board Planning with equity awards		Increasing enterprise value and stock price Accountability to shareholders, board, and management Diversification of concentrated position Expensive purchases	New or second home Venture or angel investing Strategizing goals with financial resources

Common to All Phases

Challenge	Maximize Value of Equity Awards (ISO, NQ, RSA, RSU, ESPP)
Concerns	Wealth Preservation Tax Reduction Wealth Protection Passing Assets to Heirs Charitable Giving
Solutions	Personal CFO Expert Team of Advisors Financial Education

THE PAYOFF

FOR OFFICERS OF THE COMPANY, THE ISSUES post-liquidity are different than they are for early employees. For a CEO in an IPO or acquisition situation, "it's your responsibility not only to deal with your own emotions and decisions around the liquidity event, but it's also your responsibility to make sure you are properly incentivizing and creating the atmosphere in which your team will hold together through this event and beyond," says one serial entrepreneur.[1] She advised her teams that "a liquidity event is not an end; it's the beginning."

Many startup executives and employees don't stay long at a big company if they are acquired. "The reason why you do startups is because you can't stand all of the issues surrounding big companies," says Tesla founder Marc Tarpenning. "If you end up in a big company, a startup founder or employee often decides that life is too short," and now that they have their money, they can do something else.

Kate, who we met in Phase 1, has served as general counsel for multiple startups. She remembers the challenges of day-to-day life in Phase 3. "I'm not a big-company person. I really don't like working in these big bureaucratic organizations. For each of my past acquisitions, I typically had a transition period where I had to stay in the new organization. It's been frustrating, to say the least. At one company, we had endless meetings on [their corporate philosophy]." She remembers wishing, "I just want to get some work done!" Multiple meetings on the same subject were too inefficient for this bright executive. "You can have one meeting on [corporate philosophy]. We don't need three meetings a week on it. Because it's so bureaucratic, they've been successful with [the corporate philosophy] and training everybody how to speak a certain way, and present in a certain way. Every meeting had a PowerPoint. It works for them, but that's not me."

After liquidity, if you choose to stay with the company—or if you must stay because your contract requires you to—you can expect greater accountability, and therefore more pressure from the board, shareholders, and management. Your focus may shift away from innovative technology and toward increasing the stock price. However, while you might feel some shareholder pressure at work, you may experience more flexibility in your personal life. You might also start making a few large purchases, such as a house or an extended vacation.

Now that you've earned your wealth, a financial planner can help you protect and grow it. The "Partnering with an Advisor" chapter will help to guide you through your choices, including helping you figure out if you can do it yourself.

Two Post-IPO Paths

Two general paths exist for most people in Phase 3.

MERGER OR ACQUISITION

If your company is acquired or merged, you may be required to join the acquiring firm. However, if you're in marketing or finance, your former job may be rolled up with those departments in the acquiring firm (which may be in another city), or your job may be eliminated. People often stay with the new company for a minimal amount of time to realize the vesting of stock options and to help with the company integration.

INITIAL PUBLIC OFFERING (IPO)

If your company has an IPO, you will likely stay long enough to see your low-priced options vest. Many people are optimistic about staying with the public company when they enter Phase 3, but reality soon sets in. A public company is very different than a startup. Now, you have more accountability and scrutiny.

Your life—and your planning tactics—will be slightly different depending on whether you stay after the liquidity event. Because a merger, acquisition, or

IPO produces similar financial and personal challenges, I will not distinguish between them in the discussion of Phases 3 and 4. However, there are some notable differences that I have highlighted below.

Integration, If You Stick Around

Phase 3 is an integration period. I have heard that very few senior executives stay beyond two years. One person I spoke with who had three liquidity events said that probably more than 90% of executives and employees leave within two years. In a merger or acquisition, cultural issues and financial independence usually are the forces driving people away.[2]

Now that the company has capital, it can continue to expand. The new people coming in don't have the upside that you once had. And it's hard for the early folks to keep up the same passion that they had in the early phases.

Dave Buchanan, a veteran of more than a dozen high-tech companies explains the stubbornness, thick skin, and incredible focus needed to build a successful company in Phases 1 and 2 that will help you to make it through the great divide of a liquidity event. "But they're exactly the qualities you have to learn to shed," when it comes time to preserving your wealth through the vesting period of Phase 3, says Buchanan. "You have to adapt."

If you've been through an IPO, you're working for a public company and there's much more transparency about activities and financials. New people are coming into your work family you didn't initially invite, which can be awkward. However, if you stick around, your job will include building greater enterprise value.

VESTING IN PEACE

If a merger or acquisition is the Phase 3 exit, it often means executives and employees go to work for the new or acquiring company. If you were the boss in Phase 2, it's entirely likely you won't be once you enter Phase 3. Some passionate startup people trudge through their contract terms, even if they only have to stay a year. "I waited a year and a day because I couldn't wait to get out of there. It was so stultifying! I was like part of the Borg," says one advisor, referencing the fictional alien race that assimilates other species via violence and abductions to achieve its ultimate goal of "perfection."[3] Others stay on because they have signed non-compete agreements, which forbid them from going to work for other companies operating in a similar space—often defined loosely.

Some of these people practice "VIP, vesting in peace," says VC Lara Druyan. These folks stay at the company—whether it's a new company or the same company post-IPO—and continue to vest in their stock. If there's money on the table, it's a wise wealth decision to stay and keep vesting.

ACKNOWLEDGE, CELEBRATE & PLAN

Do celebrate your achievement! While there's a tendency to relax and say, "We've made it," those responsible for building the company now have to continue to perform and keep teams motivated. Sometimes, watching the stock price is a motivator. However, with a volatile stock, the roller-coaster movement can cause the team to get excited and then depressed. This situation could become a self-fulfilling prophecy, affecting the team's work with the potential to actually impact the stock price. It takes a thoughtful CEO to continue to motivate employees through the post-liquidity phases.[4]

If you find yourself free of work responsibilities because you have no contractual obligation, now is the time to do some careful planning about your next move, advises one VC.

When and How to Leave

Employees who stay through an IPO or go to work for the acquiring company typically don't stay for long. The reasons for this short-term stay vary, but the time horizon is predictable.

Longtime Google engineer James Whittaker penned a widely circulated blog post called "Why I left Google." His main reason for leaving: the mission changed, and he no longer felt passionate about the company. Whittaker explained, "The Google I was passionate about was a technology company that empowered its employees to innovate. The Google I left was an advertising company with a single-minded corporate-mandated focus."[5] He loved the beginning, when it was an "innovation factory, empowering employees to be entrepreneurial through Founders' Awards, peer bonuses, and 20% time to innovate." (Gmail was invented in Paul Buchheit's 20% time project.[6])

Google's advertising revenue gave employees the room to think, innovate, and create. Whittaker loved showing Google off to prospective employees and giving speeches at conferences. But then, in his view, "suddenly, 20% meant half-assed. Google Labs was shut down. App Engine fees were raised." Whittaker remembers that "as the trappings of entrepreneurship were dismantled," so were "the days of old Google hiring smart people and empowering them to invent the future." Whittaker no longer felt connected to the company he had been so proud of and decided he had to go.

While a startup goes public in a burst of excitement, after some time, many of my sources recall echoing Whittaker's concerns. Their days were much less interesting and much more routine. Many early employees who weren't inspired by the change couldn't think of reasons to stay.[7]

Likewise, after a hot social media company was acquired by an iconic tech giant, some of the non-executive engineers were upset by the deal.[8] They chose to work at the small San Francisco startup to build cool technology; the idea of becoming an employee of a large company and negotiating their way through its office politics made them reconsider their careers.

Many in the startup world are motivated by the need to have a big impact, explains Rebecca Weeks Watson, VP of Business Development at RadiumOne.[9] As their companies grow (or are acquired), those with a startup mentality get frustrated with the slow speed and bureaucracy of larger organizations.[10] For many who love startup life, the larger the organization, the less fun it is.

When it comes time to leave, heed this advice from Eric Gold, an international software sales executive who has participated in multiple IPOs: "Always leave with dignity and professionalism. You run into people over and over again." He continues, "No matter how much anybody wronged you—if you got fired or somebody screwed you at work—never get angry at the people and always leave professionally and as friends. Because five to 10 years later, you won't even remember what you were mad at them about, but they'll only remember that you were an asshole."

Stay or Leave—But Don't Lose Your Wealth

Whether you stay or go, it becomes especially important to protect and preserve your wealth in Phases 3 and 4. As a longtime Silicon Valley banker says, "I've seen a lot of wealthy people lose their wealth, where they've gone from billions of dollars net worth down to $200 million overnight because they had all their [assets in one stock]. The stock market is not forgiving."[11] Thinking back to the dot-com boom days, he knew a man "who was very good at starting companies." His big home run earned him paper wealth of over $1 billion. "He was told to diversify by a prominent venture capital firm he worked with" and by many others, "and he wouldn't do it; he saw his net worth drop nearly $1 billion overnight." The entrepreneur continued to hold as the stock price dropped further and he was left with $150 million. Nothing to sneeze at, to be sure, but nothing like what he could have had had he chosen to diversify.

"Many people would think that's a lot of money," I said to the banker. He replied, "If you have a $20 million house and a $20 million wine collection and a $20 million art collection, and if you have Rolls Royces and Bentleys, then all of a sudden $150 million isn't that much money to [support this lifestyle]. I've seen VCs with a $50 million net worth, the market crashed, and they ended up having more debt than worth."

Responses to my inquiry about the positive attributes that allow people to thrive after a liquidity event varied. The Silicon Valley banker said holding on to wealth takes "not just intelligence, but also common sense." Having good role models as a child and an understanding of the value of money and how hard it is to make are helpful for preserving wealth.

PHASE 3
REALIZING THE DREAM

Post-Transition Phase
1–24 Months

The Four Phases of Startup Life[SM]

	Phase 1	Phase 2	Liquidity Event	Phase 3	Phase 4
	Pre-Transition 2-40 years **Laying the Foundation**	**Pre-Transition** 0-24 months **Ramping Up**		**Post-Transition** 1-24 months **Realizing the Dream**	**Into the Future** 2-40 years **What's Next?**
Quality of Life Challenges					
	Preoccupation with startup Loneliness Optimism Tenacity	Maintaining balance while working long hours Excitement Persistence		Weighing career options If you stay: Vest in peace and maintain work-life balance If you leave: Figure out what's next	Flexibility and choices Charitable activities Travel New career or startup Passion projects
Financial Challenges					
	Raising capital Below-market salary Accountability to investors Funnel all resources to create and build the company	Increasing enterprise value Salary and bonus Accountability to investors, management, and board Planning with equity awards		Increasing enterprise value and stock price Accountability to shareholders, board, and management Diversification of concentrated position Expensive purchases	New or second home Venture or angel investing Strategizing goals with financial resources

Common to All Phases

Challenge	Maximize Value of Equity Awards (ISO, NQ, RSA, RSU, ESPP)
Concerns	Wealth Preservation Tax Reduction Wealth Protection Passing Assets to Heirs Charitable Giving
Solutions	Personal CFO Expert Team of Advisors Financial Education

REALIZING THE DREAM

THE TIME JUST AFTER A LIQUIDITY EVENT—Phase 3—is short, and it follows a clear pattern for most people. After their equity awards vest or company integration is complete, many people leave the company. In the meantime, employees who stay post-event continue to work hard to increase the enterprise's value, although the mission may have started to change.

However, depending on your exit type, you may not experience Phase 3. If the company is acquired or merged and you're not required to stay, you may jump directly from Phase 2 to Phase 4.

If you do enter Phase 3, you will likely have stock options still vesting, and if you're lucky, vesting is accelerated. If you've gone through an IPO, there is generally a six-month lockup on selling shares. There are exceptions that enable you to get early liquidity, such as being an early employee, since you may be able to sell shares on the private secondary market.

This phase is rewarding in many ways. There's a fulfillment after the deal goes through and the realization that your hard work has paid off, both financially and emotionally.[1] But when the great sense of accomplishment subsides, or there is a lack of financial planning guidance, spending can get out of hand for some people. Immediately after the liquidity event, a tangible purchase can be satisfying. To make a statement, or just to enjoy the rewards of hard work, many sources mentioned post-wealth event purchases of an expensive car or a home. Having a written plan for your personal life is a good idea, but any plan is better than none at all.

PROFILE

CHANGING THE WAY WE DRIVE AND READ: MARTIN EBERHARD

FOUNDED TESLA MOTORS, WHOSE 2010 IPO RAISED $266 MILLION.[2]

FOUNDED NUVOMEDIA, ACQUIRED IN 2000 BY GEMSTAR-TV GUIDE.[3]

For many people in the high-tech community, the best way to approach finances is a combination of strategies: managing the parts that you have the time, energy, and knowledge to do yourself, and outsourcing the rest. Martin Eberhard is the perfect example of a financial success story.

A brilliant engineer in addition to being a successful serial entrepreneur, Eberhard is perhaps best known for his role as a founder of electric car company Tesla Motors.[4] He is boundless in his creativity and new ideas. In 1987, Eberhard helped to create Networking Computing Devices, Inc. (NCD),[5] which produced network terminals and went public in 1992.[6] Five years after NCD's IPO, Eberhard invented ebooks when he founded NuvoMedia, which was acquired by Gemstar-TV Guide in January 2000. He was such a visionary that he recalls, "when the Kindle came out, Jeff Bezos called me at home and asked me what I thought." Eberhard founded Tesla in June of 2003 and left the company three years before its June 2010 IPO.[7]

While many entrepreneurs believe so firmly in their companies that they are blind to bad news and ride their stock down to zero, Eberhard thrived financially after each liquidity event. His personal financial success lies in the fact that he had a plan: "My advice to anybody involved in a startup company is the minute you have liquidity, sell half. It's not a vote of confidence against the company to diversify. If you don't, and the stock goes down—and I've watched many, many of my friends let it ride down to zero—you're going to feel terrible. And if it goes up, you still have that other half to ride up, but you also have your nest egg." Eberhard is not as stringent with the other half. "Once I've sold half, I've taken a lot more than I put into the company," and for that Eberhard is very fortunate, since such consistent success doesn't happen as often as you might expect.

Eberhard understands that having a plan is only half the battle. To thrive, you must make sure you execute it. When NuvoMedia was acquired, he was unable to sell for six months due to his executive position. Then, the company kept him from selling shares by delaying its S-3 filing. "And so I hammered them and hammered them to get the S-3 done." He and his co-founder continued to lean on the company, resorting to legal pressure to get the filing completed. "And because I had such a bad feeling about that company, I sold all of [my stock] immediately, every single share, at the first opportunity." Eberhard's strategy paid off. "Their stock was selling at [approximately] $110 a share. By the time I could sell it, it was in the $80s, so I had lost 20 some-odd percent of the value of the stock. And by the time one of my vice presidents sold, because he didn't listen to my advice, it was at $3 a share. So he watched it go from $110 down to $3."

Eberhard showed the same tenacity when it came to selling his Tesla stock. "The minute I could sell, I sold. In fact, the day that we could sell was my wife's birthday, and we were in Maui. I was up at two in the morning selling stock as fast as I could. I sold about 90% of what I held in the first 20 minutes of trading, and bought my wife a very nice gift."

Figure 2. Martin Eberhard's Tesla. Photo taken by author, February 2, 2012.

The decision to sell is wise, but it is not always the best choice. When I met Eberhard in February 2012, selling Tesla Motors stock was a good move. However, at the time of this writing in August 2014, Tesla has sharply outperformed the S&P 500, due to large gains in the stock during 2013.[8] The comparison time period matters. As a founder, Eberhard realized tangible value from his hard work creating and building his company. He wisely preserved his wealth by selling the majority of his shares.

The other key to Eberhard's financial success is the fact that he outsources what he cannot or does not want to do himself. "I'm an engineer. I want to think about engineering; money is boring." As soon as he recognized that he wasn't going to track his personal finances each and every day, he realized it was time to hire someone who would. "Unless you're on top of the money every single day, you need to pay for somebody who is, or you're going to lose it. My portfolio is so diverse right now, and [my advisor is] constantly looking at it." His advisor also has a level of expertise that Eberhard doesn't. "It's really hard to diversify enough that you're actually diverse, not correlated, and you can't do that on your own. It's really complex, and unless you're on top of it, you're throwing your money away." Eberhard smartly understands the dangers of do-it-yourself investing.

"I don't really like playing with money very much," Eberhard explains. "But on the other hand, I do care about getting wiped out financially. A lot." His motivation for hiring an advisor is to preserve his wealth so that he can continue to start and build great companies, exercise his creative muscle, and retain his financial freedom.

Eberhard's philosophy on outsourcing extends beyond investing. "I did my own taxes with TurboTax up until NCD's IPO. Then, it was too hard. I could have done it, but it would have consumed me." Although he has a limited understanding of his taxes, Eberhard recognizes that he'd rather spend his valuable time with his family and building his businesses. Outsourcing works for him, because he trusts his advisor. "I put huge amounts of trust in my financial advisor, and it has taken me decades to build that trust. If she advises me to do something, I generally take her advice." If you don't trust your advisor, it can undermine his or her effectiveness. See the chapter on "Partnering with an Advisor at Any Phase" for tips on how to find the right advisor for you.

■ ■ ■ ■

The BE WISE Planning Strategy™

The BE WISE Planning Strategy is a formula for financial success and personal happiness before and after a startup liquidity event. To have a satisfying life, it's important to identify your passions and your goals.

I call the process of discovering and planning for life before, during, and after an IPO or other wealth event **BE WISE: Before Event, Work, Identify, Strategize, Execute**.

Before Event

Create a business plan incorporating your goals for your company and your career, which will likely include some of your personal values.

Work

Build your company. Consult with a CPA or comprehensive financial planner about tax planning with your equity awards. Entrepreneurs: Strategize the ideal corporate and equity award structure, and hire an attorney to create contracts, early exercise elections, and vesting schedules.

Identify

Identify what's important to you. How will you spend your time if your company is sold, acquired, or goes public? Don't be caught without a plan.

Strategize

Determine if your assets will support your goals and values. Carve out a "Maintain Bucket" for long-term lifestyle needs. Allocate excess capital into "Risk," "Give," and other buckets, if needed.

Execute

Implement and monitor specific action items as a road map to achieve your goals, preserve your wealth, minimize risk and taxes, and pass along assets to those you care about.

While the last two stages are chronological—your plan is analyzed, then action steps are created and executed, with or without the assistance of a financial planner—Work and Identify should happen together. For a more detailed description of the BE WISE Planning Strategy, a guide to help you plan for your personal and financial future, and a profile of a well-known entrepreneur who used it successfully, see the appendix beginning on page 175.

STRATEGIZE: MAINTAIN, RISK & GIVE

Life is expensive. If you know where you want to go, a financial plan can help you highlight any gaps that may exist along the way. After a liquidity event, you should strategize your goals and how to use your assets. The timing is important, because if you wait too long post-liquidity, you may lose out on planning and wealth-creation opportunities. Through quantitative analysis, determine if your assets will support your goals, values, and interests for the remainder of your life. If you have excess, you get to decide what to do with this pot of funds—the cherry on top.

First, list your goals. Here are some examples of short-term financial goals:

- Purchase a $2 million home in San Francisco within the next year.
- Travel around Asia next year for two months, spending $30,000.
- Protect your dependents and yourself with insurance coverage, allowing your family to continue in its existing lifestyle if an unexpected accident or illness occurs.

Some long-term financial objectives may include:

- Fund your children's four-year private university education beginning in 10 years.
- Accumulate (or preserve) funds to maintain your current lifestyle during retirement.
- Provide for your dependents and heirs.

The second step is to assess your resources and evaluate your ability to reach both your personal and financial goals. Unrealistic goals lead to frustration, and planning now to avoid disappointment later is a major component of the Strategize phase of the BE WISE Planning Strategy. Recognize that your goals will shift over time. Therefore, you should review them whenever life-changing events occur. Many independent, fee-only advisors recommend that our clients review their goals annually, at a minimum.

To protect your finances and reach these goals, divide your wealth into two or three categories, or buckets, specifically a "Maintain Bucket," a "Risk Bucket," and a "Give Bucket."

❶ The Maintain Bucket. The first bucket should consist of what you need to comfortably live out your life. This money is what you need to continue in your lifestyle; extensive analytical work, often under the guidance of a financial planner, should be done to determine this amount. Never dip into this pile for extra angel investment capital or other risky ventures. It's crucial to make sure the assets in your Maintain portfolio to fund your future are invested in a prudent, risk-appropriate way.

❷ The Risk Bucket. The second pot contains exploration funds; you can use this money for angel investing, self-managed investment portfolios, starting a new company—whatever you like. This second pot should never be merged with the first. Keeping these buckets separate should ensure that you have enough money to support your lifestyle, even if all of your Risk portfolio investments fail.

❸ The Give Bucket. If you are charitably inclined, the third pot is for making donations to your favorite causes.

Before you divide your assets into the Maintain, Risk, and Give Buckets (or more), you'll want to understand what you have, how long it will last, and how to protect it. The best way to gain a thorough understanding is to perform an analysis, preferably with an experienced and knowledgeable advisor or a qualified family member, friend, or co-worker. However, be wary of any tax implications.

If you work with a financial planner, he or she should prepare the following documents and analyses:

❶ Net Worth Statement. This document should include an inventory of your assets and liabilities. Life insurance should be accounted for here, as well. Identify whether you have adequate property and casualty insurance to protect your assets from unintended loss (from natural disasters, theft, or inattention) or from being unjustly taken in a lawsuit.

❷ Cash Flow Projection. Determines inflows and outflows of cash on an after-tax basis to show yearly surpluses or deficits. An ongoing (or large one-time) cash surplus may allow for increased spending, the ability to take on less risk in the portfolio, or earlier financial independence. A deficit requires strategizing on how best to fund your needs and how to provide a sustainable cash flow in a tax-efficient way.

❸ Financial Independence Projection. An analysis shows if your assets will allow you to achieve your goals. You may need to tweak your plan here. For example, if you want to use cash savings to invest in new companies, it's important to know how much you could afford to lose and still achieve your most important goals. This step determines how much goes to your Maintain Bucket, and how much you have left to risk or give.

❹ Insurance Analyses. Calculate how best to protect your family and your lifestyle in the event of an illness, disability, or other catastrophe.

Strategizing a plan and carving out a Maintain Bucket after your liquidity event, however, means very little if you fail to execute it. For those on the conservative side, you can invest your Maintain assets over time using a dollar cost average strategy (see tip on page 124 for details). But you need to act quickly with these decisions, because the market won't wait for you.

Comprehensive financial planning starts by examining the six basic building blocks: tax planning, cash flow analysis, long-term retirement planning, estate planning, investment planning, and insurance planning. During this process, you'll want to address each area as appropriate for you.

When you're through, you should know whether your assets will support your short- and long-term financial goals, and therefore, the total amount you need to set aside in a risk-appropriate, diversified portfolio. Likewise, you should have an idea of how costly it will be to use your excess funds (outside of your Maintain portfolio) to address your personal values, play with the stock market, invest in risky ventures, or donate to charity. (See the section on charitable giving starting on page 144 for ideas on how best to manage this portion of your portfolio.)

INVESTING CORE ASSETS CONSERVATIVELY

High-tech clients of CPA Jason Graham often work with advisors to determine the amount they need to maintain their lifestyle. Determine this core of assets—the Maintain Bucket—based on what you spend each year or, in other words, "your personal burn rate," explains Graham. "What are those assets that you want to sit there and be protected and give you peace of mind? And then, with whatever's excess, then maybe you can invest a little more aggressively.

"Bonds historically have been safe, but who knows what the future holds?" cautions Graham. "And if you don't have someone on your side who's helping you to monitor the market, monitor what's going on, rebalancing your portfolio when you need to because things can get out of whack, and where you once thought you had this safe amount set aside, that amount may no longer be safe because of changes in market conditions."

Avoid a Concentrated Position

You've now determined where you are and have a vision for where you want to be. It's crucial to make sure the assets in your Maintain portfolio are invested in a prudent, risk-appropriate way.

"The engineering community tries to be analytical but has a real emotional attachment to their particular [company] stock," says serial entrepreneur Marc Tarpenning. "They have a lot of their wealth tied up in one stock, even though any rational financial planner would say 'You've really got to hedge that, you have to diversify.'" He continues, "I've watched people over and over again ride all of that down to zero if the company doesn't do well." He and his co-founder at two successful companies "always told our employees to sell some." Their rationale: "Maybe it's going to go higher, maybe it's going to go lower, but you should get something out of it, whether it's to put a down payment on the house or buy a new car. You should do something to show how you really did. You worked on this, and you put your heart and soul into it, and you've got something out of it."

Many executives and early employees diversify a concentrated equity position, says Tarpenning, "because they want to have enough that their basic lifestyle is protected. And they can crank down that lifestyle if things get bad, but they want to make sure that they can still send the kids to school, keep the house," regardless of the market value of the one stock that gave them paper wealth. While they may end up with far greater wealth outside the Maintain Bucket, "they have that little core thing that's making sure [they can achieve their goals]. I certainly have done that. The worst thing to do is run out of money, because then it forces you to make non-optimal decisions."

Even Microsoft founder Bill Gates employed a diversification strategy early on. And no one can accuse him of not believing in his company. "Many years ago, when Microsoft was still relatively small and Bill Gates was not the richest man in the world, he sold $60 million in Microsoft stock, and it made news because it was the first time," explains Tarpenning. "I figure that even Bill Gates, who was worth hundreds of millions of dollars at the time, was hedging his bets, just in case."

Billionaire high-tech veteran Eric Schmidt, who reigned as Google's CEO for 10 years and stepped down in April 2011, also adopted a diversification strategy.[9] Though he's still committed to the company, serving as executive chairman, the *Wall Street Journal* reported Schmidt filed to sell 40% of his Google stock, or 3.2 million shares, in 2013 and early 2014. As of November 2013, the 3.2 million shares he planned to sell were valued at $2.5 billion.[10] After the sale, his personal exposure to the stock of Google would decrease by more than half over two years. In a statement from the company, Schmidt's plan was described "as part of his long-term strategy for individual asset diversification and liquidity."[11]

DON'T BET ON YOUR COMPANY'S STOCK

An executive responsible for educating the employees of her startup about equity awards before and after the liquidity event related a story of failure.[12] Several years ago, a very bright lawyer friend of hers got fearful about exercising his options and selling his company stock. "He refused to sell any stock, because he felt like that would mean that he didn't believe in the company. And then he lost everything. It's really unfortunate. The stock price kept going down, down, down, and he wouldn't diversify and wouldn't diversify, and he literally got nothing. And it's sad. He's got two kids. He doesn't own a home. But he wouldn't listen to any advice on diversifying."

When asked about the major financial challenges on a personal level that individuals who go through a liquidity event face, IPO consultant Lise Buyer replied, "Figuring out how to manage your finances when they're often concentrated in a single security or a single industry, and one that is historically—and likely to continue to be—very volatile. That's number one. Number two," she continued, "is we in Silicon Valley are a very optimistic bunch. Our stocks won't go down. That's a challenge, recognizing that you can't top tick [the market]. You will almost always sell at the 'wrong' time, but you still need to [sell]. "And number three," Buyer concluded, "is that technology can become obsolete, and no one is ever prepared for that."

Fast-talking and fast-thinking Buyer has experienced a big liquidity event herself and offers her best advice for making smart decisions after options and equity awards vest: "Be pragmatic. Stocks go up, and stocks go down. No stock—not Apple, not Google, not Facebook, not Microsoft, not Intel—always goes up. [It may go] up for a while, and come down, and nobody's good enough to pick the top. Be rational, be pragmatic, diversify."

Diversification starts with selling company stock, but shouldn't end there. Strategic diversification spreads your investments between many companies, in many parts of the world, so you avoid putting all of your eggs in one basket. Concentration is the opposite of diversification. It's what happens when you fail to take action to sell your company stock. It makes sense to take enough off the table to ensure your most important goals are met, including maintaining your lifestyle and perhaps college education for your children.

Investing in a diversified portfolio is a less risky way to achieve your goals than owning one stock—even (perhaps especially) if that one stock is where you work.

DON'T LET THE TAX TAIL WAG THE DOG

Taxes paralyze some people and cause them to make poor investment decisions. Yet, "If you have to pay taxes, it means you're making money," says a multi-decade high-tech veteran. "There was one year that I wrote a check to the IRS for, like, $700,000, and I was complaining to my brother. And he goes, 'If you owe them that much money, I'm not crying for you.'"[13]

Sitting on Cash

CPA Jason Graham has seen some clients hesitate to diversify after a liquidity event. He thinks maybe it's because they're still remembering the market volatility of 2008. These clients will cash out, "and then they'll go out and buy a home, or they'll buy a bigger home, or they'll go on an expensive honeymoon." With the remainder of their liquidity, "they're a bit gun-shy to get it out working for them in the marketplace. And so they'll just sit on it in cash."

While they will often sell out of a concentrated company stock position, it won't be into something that will grow and provide for their future. "Part of it is taking the time to figure out what they want to do with it. To either figure it out on their own or engage an investment advisor to guide them along the way. Because they're hesitant to take that next step [to diversify into a portfolio], and they're so focused on the next thing [their next company], they're not necessarily losing money, so to speak, but it's not growing for them," says Graham. Nor is the cash keeping up with inflation.

Holding Company Stock: Set Targets and Triggers

When asked if she understood the risk consequences to holding equity awards such as restricted stock and options, an ex-Googler replied thoughtfully, "There's a difference there between rationally understanding it, and *emotionally* understanding it." If the stock price goes down, that's real wealth lost. Emotionally, it's harder to contemplate the downside and diversify out of your own company stock if it's rising.[14]

Setting price targets and time triggers on your company stock allows you to have a rational plan. Analysis can determine a price target on the downside, to identify the lowest point at which to sell whereby you can still maintain your financial independence. By establishing a 10b5-1 plan with your employer to sell a predetermined number of shares on a set schedule, such as when you vest (see the 10b5-1 section on page 122), company insiders may trade stock even when they would otherwise be in a blackout period, thus avoiding insider trading restrictions. Having a 10b5-1 plan will keep you in compliance of the law, while minimizing your risk of concentration in the stock of your company. It also enables you to be disciplined, rather than purely reactive, emotional, or even helpless when and if the stock price changes. (And it will.)

When you determine what you need to achieve financial independence, secure just this amount in a diversified portfolio. Then, you can regard the rest of your company stock as your "risk capital," which you can hold until it reaches your price targets—or even, forever.

PROFILE

THE DOWNSIDE OF ENTHUSIASM: ROBERT CARTER

EXECUTIVE AT NUVOMEDIA, WHICH WAS ACQUIRED IN 2000 BY GEMSTAR-TV GUIDE.[15]

> Nearly everyone I spoke with for this book personally knows someone who worked for a startup that was acquired, merged, or went public and subsequently lost everything due to poor planning.
>
> A native New Yorker, Robert Carter was introduced to the Bay Area founders of ebook company NuvoMedia in the pre-Kindle late 1990s.[16] Carter was hired as a corporate development consultant and soon became the Senior VP of Content and Business Development.[17] Through perseverance and savvy sales skills, he acquired content and signed big-name publishers to use ebooks before they even existed in the public consciousness. Carter participated in the deal that saw NuvoMedia acquired by Gemstar-TV Guide in 2000 for $180 million in stock.[18] He received stock options in return for his hard

work, which at one point composed up to 90% of his net worth.

Carter was extremely optimistic about where his company stock was headed: "I found my mind was very geared towards supporting a thesis that the stock would hold up: nine [analysts] had a 'Strong Buy' [rating] on Gemstar-TV Guide, and somebody described [the CEO] being 'as tough as John Malone, as smart as Bill Gates, and as creative as Steve Jobs,' so I think I gravitated towards those comments as opposed to seeing that he seemed to have an unusual relationship with the CFO and had about 100 direct reports!"

Though Carter was advised to "dump half" of his holdings in the acquiring company right away, he wanted to wait a year to sell at the reduced long-term capital gain tax rate. So he held on. He watched his net worth go up and down. The deal was done at $55, per share, and the stock immediately shot up to $107. "And then it dropped like a stone on some loss litigation, and then went to $40, and then it rallied up to $70. It was not one of those things like a straight, diagonal drop, where you could figure out 'it's going down [and I should] get out.' It just kept [moving] in a way that would get you comfortable that it had stabilized, or is going [to go] back up. I remember refreshing the Gemstar price 15 times a day on Yahoo."

Of course hindsight is 20/20, but all the indicators signaling that the company was in trouble were there. In addition to his diminished view of the Gemstar CEO, Carter recalls visiting him on a Sunday and he was "jam-packed with activity, meaning he was working 24/7. Not a good sign." Around earnings-reporting time, "he disappeared entirely." Even when the company's executive vice president and general counsel sold all of his shares and left the company, Carter didn't think to cash out. "I should have looked at that, at that point—but, of course, you don't quite absorb it," he recalls. "This is a classic case where you just need to turn [personal financial management] over to somebody who's totally dispassionate and rational," because, "you're too emotional about it." (Hindsight, in this case, is especially telling. The CEO and CFO were also investigated for committing securities fraud.[19] The Gemstar CFO, Elsie Leung, settled in February 2006, paying a judgment of more than $1.3 million. The plea bargain for Henry Yuen, Gemstar's CEO, was rejected by the judge for being "too lenient." (Yuen was later convicted of securities fraud for misrepresenting corporate revenue and lying to auditors.)

The emotions surrounding your company stock can be powerful blinders.

Lessons Learned from Optimism

Many people I interviewed remembered making at least one mistake the first time they went through a liquidity event, mainly due to inexperience. Unfortunately for the optimistic Carter, his mistake affected more than 80% of his net worth.

Many of my sources for this book agreed that the qualities that make a successful early employee or entrepreneur are the worst traits for managing money. As a startup employee, you must be optimistic in the face of negativity from others who don't understand your project. You are putting your eggs in one basket for as long as it takes to build your company. This is highly risky behavior, and you have to be passionate about your creation to continue. After your liquidity event, you must learn a new set of skills for managing your wealth—or you should outsource this task. Skills that make for a successful money manager and a great investment experience are rationality, skepticism, and a dispassionate demeanor. How easy is it to turn passion—for a company or a stock—into objectivity for that same company or the stock of an acquiring company after you've had a successful exit?

Going on a Phase 3 Spending Spree

In my interviews, I heard a similar story again and again about how financial decisions made without considering the "fat tails" tend to have considerable negative impact.

It goes something like this: After a big IPO or other liquidity event, a successful person—worth a lot on paper—buys an expensive home. Why should they worry when their company is shooting for the moon and they are worth millions (on paper)? Soon, the company's stock starts to slip and they have not yet diversified. When the company goes under or the stock languishes long enough, they're left with the house, the mortgage payments, the tax bill, and no income stream or rising stock price to support their lifestyle.

SAVED BY A BOAT

Oddly enough, one extravagant post-IPO purchase ended up *saving* a dot-com entrepreneur from total financial loss. The founder had $100 million in paper wealth at one point. Not wanting to sell any stock, he borrowed millions to buy a giant house. He also bought a $10 million yacht. But you can't finance a yacht, so he had to sell some of his shares to pay for it. It turns out that this was the best thing that could have happened to him. He had a great time and threw huge parties, and then, his world fell apart. The company went out of business, and his stock wealth went away. He lost his house and his Flexjet card. He realized the only actual asset he had was the boat; he sold the boat, and that $7 million is what allowed him to survive and go on to his next venture. "I love boats," he said, according to my source for this story. In this man's case, an extravagant purchase actually saved his financial life. Lucky break.

The tendency in Silicon Valley is toward optimism. When your company is doing well, you are on top of your career, and your stock keeps rising, it is easy to defer saving for your future. But the unexpected can happen, and quickly. It turns out that for those who have not achieved financial independence, saving now—during your peak earning years—puts you in a much stronger position later on. A home purchase too rich for your situation can disrupt your dreams and jeopardize, if not shatter, your ability to retire on time.

To thrive after a liquidity event, it's important to keep a level head. Understanding your financial situation, and what you really can afford and not afford, is key. In the days just after a much-hyped IPO, a former employee remembers, "There were people who, before the day they had sold, they had already run up tens of thousands of dollars on their credit card, in anticipation of rewarding themselves and being able to sell. If the stock had just tanked the next day, they would have been toast."[20]

The last thing you want to do is have to work when you're physically ready to stop. Enthusiasm is rampant in the startup world and powers the quest to build and grow cool technology companies. But all financial plans should include a bit of wisdom and forethought about the very real downside risk.

What steps are you taking today to ensure your financial plan will lead you to your dream reality?

What Paralyzes People—Fear or Greed?

Primal human emotions include fear and greed. Back when we were cave dwellers, when we saw a bear, we ran away as fast as we could. Acting on our emotions in this case was very productive. Today, when we fear stocks are going down because of a bad economic report, or because stocks were down yesterday (which could be a sign of a bear market, or not), reacting based on our emotions is often a terrible thing. Because buying low and selling high is very hard to do, it's important to remove emotion from investing decisions.

But emotions are so ingrained within us, that it's very hard to always be rational when it comes to your own savings.

"When do I sell?" was the burning question on the minds of employees of a hot tech startup after their post-IPO blackout period ended. Watching the stock price during the day back then, "I remember people focused on trying to get two cents per share more before pulling the sell trigger, because that will make a huge difference," says an early employee.[21]

WHY DO THEY HOLD?

Once the lockup period ends—and in certain cases, earlier—those involved in a startup have the ability to sell their company stock and escape from a concentrated position. But I've heard and seen in practice that this logical move often does not occur. Some people never get around to selling, and they continue to hold on to their hard-won reward even as the stock value shrivels up.

To find out what motivates this decision to hold, I asked my sources: What paralyzes people, fear or greed? Do people hold on to company stock because they are afraid to miss an opportunity, or because they are greedy with the prospect of the stock price increasing?

The result: an even and overwhelming split between greed alone and a combination of both fear and greed.

Fear and Greed

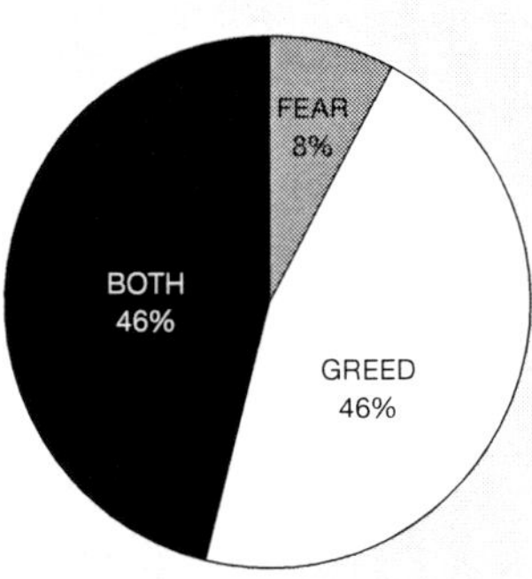

Figure 3. The chart above factors in responses from 35 interviewees.

Many people refused to even talk in these terms. Fear and greed, they argued, had too many negative connotations. Instead, they said that fear was "worry" about the alternative use of the sales proceeds, and greed was "optimism" or "enthusiasm" for the company they've helped to build. Those who could not decide between the two often replied "both," because worrying about losing out on future appreciation felt the same to them as enthusiasm for the company.

Some interviewees simply couldn't identify the emotions involved, and some avoided the question entirely. Whatever truly motivates people to hold on to their company stock, one thing is clear: investment decisions should be rational, but emotions clearly get in the way.

One former executive of a large tech company who has experienced multiple successful liquidity events prefers to describe the emotion of enthusiasm as "belief," as in, "I believe so much in this company, our stock can only go up. Is that greed or is that passion?"[22] What gets people into trouble if they are not careful, said the executive, who requested privacy, is "a belief that things only go up, and not being realistic about how quickly they can come down again." In the late 1990s while at one tech company, the stock "went up five times in the next couple of years. It was the peak of the bubble, and we had employees who didn't do any diversification because they just were sure that it was going to go up, and up, and up. And then the whole market came crashing down. There were a handful of employees that ended up just holding on, and then when it started to go down, they said, 'We're not going to sell as it's going down,' and they ended up just leaving a lot of money on the table because they were optimizing for the most." That's the problem with "anchoring" on a historical stock price that may never be reached again.

It's impossible to determine the right time to sell, and the executive acknowledged the balance between believing in your company, and therefore holding on to all of your stock, and avoiding selling out too early. It's important to understand that "even if the company does great, there are outside forces that make markets very volatile, and diversification is very important. You're so emotionally attached to your company."[23] Even analytical engineers can have an emotional attachment to their stock.

For executives, selling company stock involves legal issues. The stock transactions of executives and board members of public companies are visible to the public. One executive I spoke with who serves on boards of two Fortune 500 companies receives stock as compensation for being a director and is mindful that selling stock should be done "in a smart, ethical way. If you're a CEO or an officer of a company, you just can't diversify" without understanding and legally complying with the rules of insider trading.[24] Refer to the section on 10b5-1 plans for legal ways that insiders can avoid selling restrictions.

SELLING STOCK TO PRESERVE YOUR WEALTH

I heard a similar version of the following story multiple times: A big problem in the dot-com boom days was "selling stock thinking that you'll be able to sell more stock to pay for the taxes on the stock just sold. Then, spending the proceeds of the sale. When tax time comes around, and the remaining stock is not worth as much as you expected," it's a big shocker. "The pitfall, when you finally get to exercise or sell options, is not putting away a tax reserve. Thinking that you'll be able to fund the taxes when tax time comes around, is a very, very dangerous thing."[25]

MANAGING YOUR EMOTIONS

Emotions get in the way of rational decision making when it comes to your company's stock price. "The problem is this," said Eric Gold, an assertive executive who believes that it's easy to get caught up in company hype.[26] "You're already working for the company, that's risk enough. You don't also have to be holding stock in the company, so just get out. I'm sure there's a chance you might shoot yourself in the foot and say, 'Oh, gosh, it was the next Microsoft!'

But that's rare. And even if you sell, you're still going to be making money. You just wouldn't have made boatloads of money. The biggest mistake I made in Phase 3," Gold confessed, "was holding the stock for too long. And I learned that lesson on the first IPO."

Gold's advice after experience with two successful liquidity events echoes others I spoke with: "Sell half of it as soon as you can. Then sell another 20 to 25% when it goes up a little bit, and maybe hold it and ride 25% down. But it's only going to go down. There's nothing like the investor excitement that occurs at the IPO. Once the executives cash out, and [the investors] cash out, it's like a balloon deflating. Maybe in a few years it'll come back. But you should really just get out."

Venture capitalist Sonja Hoel Perkins, who spends her days researching and investing in companies for inclusion in her firm's investment portfolio would agree. When friends or clients have asked her over the years how much of the stock in their companies they should hold, she puts the question back to them and asks, "Would you buy that stock today?"

HOW GOOGLE MONITORED PHASE 3 GREED

GOOGLE DEALT WITH GREED JUST AFTER THE IPO IN A SUCCESSFUL WAY.

In his book *In The Plex*, author Steven Levy relays this story:

"On the day of the IPO, Wayne Rosing, the head of engineering, addressed an all-hands meeting. In his hand he held a baseball bat. He told the Googlers that if he looked in the parking lot in the next few days and saw new BMWs or Porsches, he would use the bat to smash the windshields.

"Marissa Mayer told her team that she didn't want them checking the stock price during the day. When her workers did not respond with full compliance, she instituted another policy: If anyone who worked for her spotted someone else in the group looking at the stock ticker, all he or she had to do was walk over and tap that person on the shoulder. Then that person would have to buy you a share of stock. After a number of involuntary exchanges, people either stopped checking or learned to hide their peeking more effectively."[27]

Depending upon when Google employees started, there could be a big divide between one employee's wealth and that of others on the same team. Levy's book explains:

"Even the Google masseuse noticed the impact of money, especially when it came to the divide between early employees holding valuable options and those who came later. 'While one was looking at local movie times on his monitor, the other was booking a flight to Belize for the weekend,' she wrote in her book. 'Don't think everyone wasn't aware of the rift.'"[28]

What we learn from Google is that individual outcomes exist on a spectrum. If you hold shares from your exit and don't diversify them, you could be worth many multiples of those shares in the future. You can buy a Gulfstream. Or if you continue to hold the shares and the price plummets, the corporate jet in your future might be Southwest Airlines. You just don't know. Most people tend to be optimistic and expect to be in the upside camp. But a lot can happen, and it's fraught with risk. "Even if you don't care about it personally," says one executive, you should mitigate your risk "for your family and community."

■ ■ ■ ■

GETTING WHIPSAWED

Emotional investing can get you in trouble. Mike (not his real name)[29] is an engineer whose first job was at a startup less than a year before its IPO. At the time, he didn't comprehend what an IPO was, he just needed a job. There were 20 engineers when he joined, and in addition to doing exciting work together, the tight team bonded over lunch every day at the little deli around the corner.

"[It] was a really fun place to work from an engineering point of view. We did good work. I got to work with some good engineers, and with people that founded the company. And I was mainly focused on doing the job."

On the day he started working, Mike received stock option grants. He remembers thinking, "'What do I do with this? I don't even know what this is.' I was completely naïve."

When the company went public, Mike realized his options were valuable. When his options vested a year after he started, he sold all of the shares at a profit of about $10,000. Then, he watched the price of his company's stock continue to rise exponentially. The company became one of the dot-com darlings of the late 1990s, and in hindsight Mike regrets selling all of his shares from that first vesting milestone. To balance his regret about selling in the early days, he implemented a new strategy: buying his options on margin. In the late '90s as the stock price moved up quickly, he exercised his non-qualified stock options as soon as they vested, using margin to pay for both the shares and the tax due. He held the shares in hopes of reducing taxes, because selling shares held for at least a year means paying tax at a lower rate, as long as the stock price is rising.

It was a great strategy for several years as his company's stock price continued to rise. "The gain on the stock price was way better than the cost of margin interest. The 7% margin interest cost was noise," Mike recalls. Then, the price of tech stocks began to implode. Day by day, the price of his shares dropped. He realized he'd have to sell to prevent a margin call.

"For most people coming in as a junior engineer, the real challenge is, 'How do I participate in the upside but limit the downside?'" Mike explains. Diversification is an emotional challenge when the stock price is rising. "My plan was, at the end of each year just sell a [year's worth of vested shares]. But after a while you go, 'Why would I sell this now?'" In his attempt to be analytical about diversification, he acknowledges, "If the ramp is going up, you need to participate in that. And that's where you need to be a disciplined seller."

As logical as it seemed, Mike's diversification plan failed him. He sold enough to cover all the margin loans, but was still holding as the stock price continued to dive. He recalls thinking, "'Oh, I've got everything covered, great, I'll sit here for a while.' And the stock goes down [further] and you go, 'Oh, that's not good, well I better sell some [more].' You sell on the way down."

> *Investopedia* defines "whipsaw" as: A condition where a security's price heads in one direction, but then is followed quickly by a movement in the opposite direction. The origin of [the] term is derived from the push-and-pull action used by lumberjacks to cut wood with a type of saw with the same name.[30]

Failing to participate on the upside with the first of his shares that vested, Mike admits he got greedy in later years. Looking back to the days when the stock price was falling, he wishes he had put a stop loss order on his inventory of shares. "You have to pick a price, and when it gets to that price, sell it," he says. "I'm not a good enough investor to be unemotional about it.

"If you work at a company with phenomenal growth," adds Mike, who has become financially wiser over the years, "you can do well—much better than the [stock] market. The issue is, how do you know when it's over?" He wishes he had heeded his own advice: come up with two targets—a growth rate and downside price—and sell when the growth fails to meet your target rate, or the stock price hits the downside price point. Mike urges others to look at analytical measures of growth, as opposed to a gut feeling about the company.

Finally, "after I had given back too much," Mike says with a hearty laugh, he decided to outsource the management of his personal finances. After years of following the disappointing advice from about 10 stockbrokers "pushing products" he felt were bad, he finally consolidated everything with one advisor. "I felt she was honest," Mike explains. (And she keeps him diversified.)

Decision Tree Analysis: A Rational Approach to a Concentrated Equity Position

How do you overcome your emotions about your company stock and decide if—and how much—to diversify? A Decision Tree Analysis can provide a quantitative—and rational—perspective on when and how much stock to sell.

As Mike's story demonstrates, it is often incredibly difficult to make rational decisions concerning your newly acquired wealth. If you are an analytical type and hold in-the-money options or a concentrated stock position, then a decision tree using probability analysis is a valuable way to assess your best course of action. This tool is much more helpful than basing your sell or hold decision on gut feeling.

Individuals and companies use decision trees to help understand how to evaluate risk and ambiguity. People often make non-optimal decisions when they adopt a skewed perception of their choices. In the case of a concentrated equity position, overconfidence and the enthusiasm that accompanies a recent success can cloud decisions. The decision tree combats this uncertainty by providing a clear and logical set of outcomes for a participant to choose from, based ingeniously on probabilities assigned by the participant. Assigning probabilities to each outcome and following the logical progression of each decision point can be an eye-opening exercise, especially for an analytical engineer.

THE DECISION TREE: HOW IT WORKS

This decision tree format comes originally from the Stanford Decision Analysis graduate program. The sample decision tree was created by engineer, entrepreneur, CEO, and investor Peter Herz to be used by someone holding a concentrated equity position.[31] Let's call the equity holder in this example "John." John holds a concentrated position in stock options, founders' stock, or pre-IPO shares. To create the tree, John would first populate all values in the top left corner of the graphic that have a light gray background: the number of shares he owns (500,000), his cost per share ($5), and the current trading price of the stock ($70). Second, he assigns a dollar value threshold for how much the stock must be worth in order for him to consider it a "great stock," "good stock," "mediocre stock," or "big bummer."

John then determines the subjective values, namely the future stock price and the relative percentage likelihood of the stock reaching the specific outcomes. The analytically minded Herz explains the tree matter-of-factly: "The way decision trees work is the square is a decision point, the circles are events with probabilistic outcome paths, and the triangles are endpoints. If you sell everything, you go straight to an endpoint. If you either sell half or hold all, you're then at a place where there will be a probabilistic outcome depending on what happens to the stock. And the way I set it up, I actually make the probability of the big bummer whatever's left after you divide up the odds for the great stock, the good stock, and the mediocre stock outcomes. And that helps, because then [the participant holding the concentrated position] doesn't have to think about the big bummer, and it just ends up being whatever it is." The three dollar values in the middle column are the probability-weighted outcomes of each path, ranging from $32.5 million of cash in the "sell all" scenario to $28 million of stock in the "hold all" scenario.

Herz believes it's really important that the person who has the shares and decisions to make is the person who assigns the probabilities. "If you change the [probabilities or future stock price values], it could be that one of these other

Sample Decision Tree

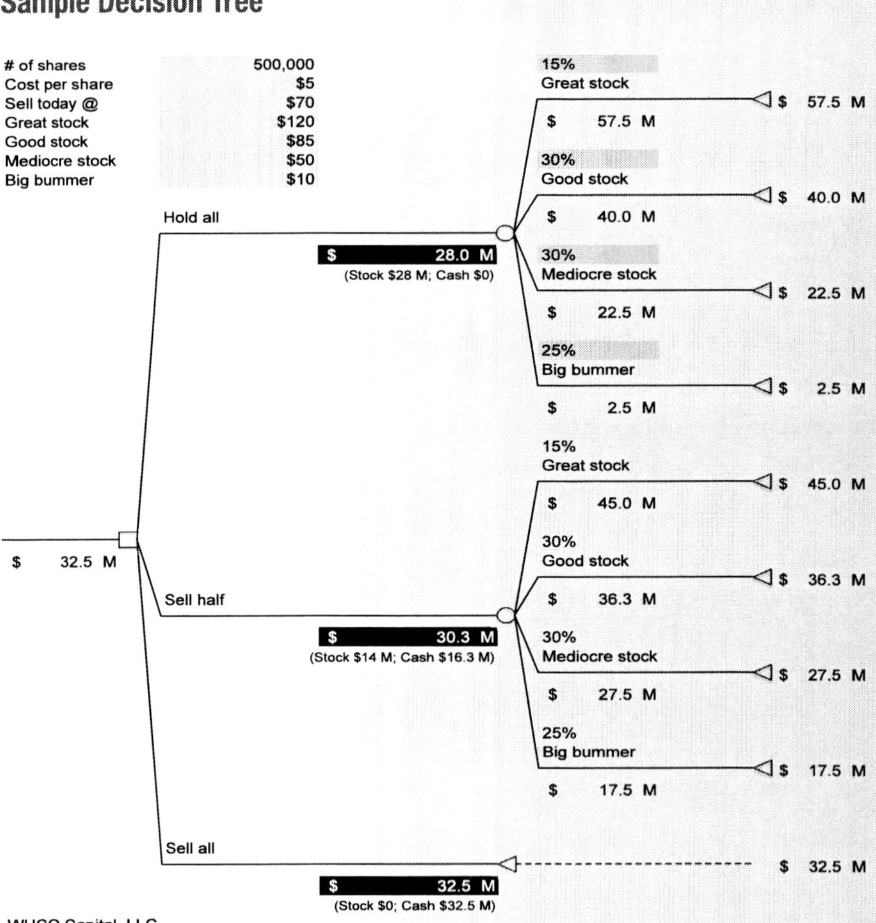

Figure 4. Sample of a completed decision tree.

paths ends up being the best path, and that number inherits whatever the best of these three paths are."

The focus of the decision tree is to avoid the chance of the worst possible outcome. "No matter how unlikely you think that probability is, you don't want to be on that [branch] of the decision tree" that will produce a catastrophic outcome. He points to the "hold all" branch explaining, "If you don't pick this path of the tree, you will never get there," pointing to the "big bummer" result of $2.5 million (a bad result in this case, only because of what the other, better choices could have returned). Herz then acknowledges this strategy also eliminates the best outcome, in which John holds everything and the stock price shoots up. "By designing out [the part of the tree with the worst result], you are leaving [a potentially] huge outcome on the table, but you're also eliminating the crap-tastic outcome of losing almost everything."

Herz applies an unemotional broad-brushstroke view to his personal startup equity. "I, as a rule, sell half, and that way I'm always half-right, and also half-wrong." His takeaway message: if you're not on "the branch that says you're holding everything, you can never get to the lose everything [result]."

THE DECISION TREE MECHANICS

The probabilities in each branch must total 100%, because there is a 100% certainty that the stock price will exist in one of these ranges. However, the price could be higher than the great stock price or lower than the big bummer price. But since the future is unknown, John is guessing when he assigns the probabilities to his tree. For example, at a stock price of $70, John thinks there is a 15% chance of the stock being great and reaching $120 per share, a 30% chance of it being good and reaching $85 per share, a 30% chance of it being mediocre and dropping to $50 per share, and a 25% chance of it being a "big bummer" and plummeting to $10 per share.

The values to the right of the triangles represent John's potential sale outcomes, which range from $2.5 million to $57.5 million. Because the first branch holds the highest outcome, it's tempting to immediately gravitate toward the "hold all" option. However, take a look at the two bottom black rectangles of the middle column. These are the "expected values" of each branch, or simply the sum of all the smaller branches to the right of the circles (sale price less cost per share, multiplied by the assigned probability in that branch), the average return John can expect to make. In the "hold all" branch, the expected value is calculated as follows:

$$\text{Expected Value} = \$28,000,000$$
$$= (\$57,500,000 \times .15) + (\$40,000,000 \times .30) +$$
$$(\$22,500,000 \times .30) + (\$2,500,000 \times .25)$$

Given the information John knows today, by holding all of his stock he can expect it will be worth $28 million. Yet two of the "hold all" branches would give him a worse result than this, and the stock price could drop (or increase) at any moment. Herz further explains that $28 million "should then be compared to the expected value of the other branches. The optimal value is the number that's ultimately shown all the way to the left [$32.5 million]; the path that produces [$32.5 million] is the path or paths that have that value in the middle column." It is the "sell all" scenario in this example that leads to the highest expected value.

Depending on the assigned probabilities, John could end up with a better outcome on the "sell half" or "hold all" branches of the tree. "For example," says Herz, if John decides "the great stock outcome has a 35% probability and [the] big bummer only a 5% probability, then 'hold all' becomes the best economic choice." Of course, the value of held shares can change at any moment.

APPLYING THE DECISION TREE
TO YOUR CONCENTRATED STOCK OR OPTION POSITION

The decision tree is a valuable tool to use in conjunction with the BE WISE Planning Strategy for identifying your goals and strategizing how best to deploy assets (see page 175). If you're holding a concentrated position, this rational approach to assessing the probability of each outcome is an eye-opening way to determine the best course of action. It's a dramatically easy means of giving you valuable perspective on your choices.

Hire a Professional Advisor or Do It Yourself?

After a liquidity event, you have an important decision to make. Will you manage your finances yourself or outsource them?

Many professional engineers and executives are very talented within their niche. They are smart and some even enjoy considering their investment options. When it comes to outsourcing their investment management, they ask, "What is an advisor going to do for me that I can't do by myself?"

Long-term investing takes willpower, patience, and the ability to ignore shouts from the talking heads on cable. Unless you're a day trader, your investments are for future needs, such as lifestyle maintenance later in life. Any cash needed in the short term (less than five years) should not be invested in the stock market. The growth in your portfolio will allow you to achieve your goals far into the future, so you can continue to live just like you do now, with no reduction in spending or lifestyle.

The advisor who takes a personalized approach is looking at your situation continually, via your portfolio and your life, to guide you when you have a change in job, marital status, family status, and the like. A good advisor will be up-to-date on tax laws, investing tools, and research—items that constantly change. If you are dedicated to your job, the only time you may have to focus on your portfolio is between 11 p.m. and 2 a.m., after you stop working for the day. Are you at your peak performance to be handling your financial future at that time? Can you be sure you'll take action when you need to, to trade in order to harvest tax losses, convert to a Roth IRA when your income is low (and the market may be low, which feels like a scary time), or purchase adequate insurance to protect your net worth?

> "From my perspective, why we hired an advisor is to look at it continually, not in a 2 to 4 a.m. window," says one recently retired executive. The advisor is "looking at our situation and seeing what may be happening in the world, filtered to our particular situation. A Google search gives me a barrage of the top news stories for one topic, but without a customized filter."[32]

Technologists are trained experts in a particular area, but they may not be able to answer detailed questions outside of their niche. The technical spectrum is only so wide for most people. Financial planning is equally nuanced. Your advisor should have a network of unbiased resources to help you. However, be cautious of financial planners who tell you they can handle all of your needs—including insurance—in-house, as there may be conflicts of interest.

With the right advisor, the benefits should outweigh the costs in management fees. However, if you have the time, interest, and skill set to manage your new wealth, then being your own financial planner might make sense.

If you're not sure where you fall on the DIY versus outsource spectrum, read on for tips to help you make an informed decision. And if you already know you don't want to spend the time or energy checking the markets daily and strategizing your financial life, turn to page 157 for guidance on partnering with a financial advisor and page 160 for a guide to finding the right advisor.

CAN YOU DO YOUR OWN FINANCIAL PLANNING?

Online personal finance software, magazines, and self-help books claim to guide you in your financial planning. However, you may decide to seek help from a professional financial planner if:

- You lack expertise in certain areas of your financial picture, such as college savings plans, wealth protection, tax planning, charitable giving, or retirement projections due to changing family circumstances.
- You want a professional second opinion about the financial plan you have developed for yourself.
- You don't have the time to do your own financial planning.
- You have an immediate need for assistance, or an unexpected life event such as a birth, inheritance, or major illness.[33]

"The biggest pitfall" about personal financial management, says Yahoo CFO Ken Goldman, "is that you get overconfident. You don't create enough breathing room in your cash, so you go right to the cliff and you maybe jump off because you haven't [got enough]. I've seen people who just don't pay enough attention."[34]

FIVE DECISIONS TO MAKE ABOUT INVESTING

In *The Investment Answer*, Daniel Goldie and Gordon Murray list five decisions you must make if you're thinking of taking charge of your own investing.[35] I've summarized each below and expanded on the rebalancing piece:

❶ **The Do-It-Yourself Decision**—Do you have the time and interest to manage your own finances? Does the money you save on professional management make up for the returns you may be missing out on?

❷ **The Asset Allocation Decision**—What percentage of volatile stocks to volatility-dampening bonds should you choose? How much downside can you handle on a day-to-day basis in order to meet your needs later in life? Are you aware of how to boost long-term returns, such as by adding small-cap stocks and value stocks to your mix, which have historically outperformed large-cap and growth stocks?

❸ **The Diversification Decision**—Holding many asset classes lowers your overall portfolio risk, and in most investing environments will protect you on the downside. How will you diversify?

❹ **The Active vs. Passive Decision**—Active management means using available information about the economy, specific industries, and companies to take advantage of mispriced stocks. Passive or index investing believes all available information is already reflected in the price of a stock. Which should you choose?

❺ **The Rebalancing Decision**—Since returns don't come nice and steady, asset classes in your portfolio will not move in lockstep. Independent of Goldie's view, research by Gobind Daryanani demonstrates that when an asset class moves outside of a 20% band higher or lower than the target set for that position, the trading fees are mitigated by the benefit of getting your portfolio back to target. (To understand the concept of a "band," think about a rubber band stretching, but not so far that it breaks. For example, if your target for large-cap U.S. stocks is 30% and you have a 20% band, you would rebalance when the allocation drops below 24% or rises above 36%.)[36] The important principle here is to make time to review your portfolio for asset classes that have moved far beyond their targets, and pull the trigger to rebalance.

HOW TO BE YOUR OWN FINANCIAL PLANNER: IMPLEMENT, MONITOR & ACT

Wealth planners devoted to helping clients make smart choices and achieve their dreams believe that everyone can benefit from the services of an advisor, even if it's just for a yearly checkup. But if you're a DIY person, you may want to be your own financial planner.

If so, make sure you carve out enough time on a quarterly basis, at least (or a daily basis, if you hold individual stocks), to review and research investments, monitor your holdings, add surplus cash to your portfolio, and rebalance as needed. Write down your life goals, including the cost and the time period of any expense. Then, annually review and update your goals to make sure that your priorities reflect any changes in your life. It's important to follow through on action items in a timely manner. Being your own financial planner requires you to look at the big picture as well as the details, to keep yourself on track to achieve your goals.

While research[37] shows that working with an impartial, knowledgeable financial professional can set you and your family up for greater success—financial and otherwise—for the rest of your life, it is possible to go it alone. In fact, an early Google employee says this about the many brilliant engineers she knows who are investing DIYers: "I think a lot of them actually do a fine job."[38] They read a few publications or do web research and "put their dollars in a diversified portfolio, and they go ahead and let it ride. It might not be optimized, it might not be as much [as they could earn with an advisor], but it's hard to tell what would have been." The ex-Googler, who uses an advisor herself, paraphrases these DIYers: "I'd rather know what I know and have myself make the mistakes, rather than pay someone X dollars, when I don't know how much better they would have been able to do."

I know the type. My engineer brother talks to me about his stocks and mutual funds on holidays and summer vacations. He knows about the benefits of tax loss harvesting but doesn't make the time to actively review his portfolio on a regular basis. One December, I happened to see him just before the last trading day of a particularly volatile year for stocks. We got to talking about the losses in his portfolio, and I suggested that he realize the tax loss on paper by selling a handful of funds before the end of the year. He did, but without prompting from me, he would have lost that opportunity—and the thousands of dollars in taxes it saved him.

PROFILE

EVAN'S STORY: MISSING THE BIG PICTURE

HOW TO FIND THE HOLES IN YOUR PLAN.

"I just don't have time to tax plan," says Evan (not his real name),[39] an executive who was recently part of an acquisition. "I work 20 hours a day. And so to me, to spend any amount of time outside of that focused on optimizing dollars is really ridiculous. That's because I have the philosophy that I have to enjoy my life. I don't want to lose sleep over worrying about dollars and cents, if I know that what I have done so far has worked and it's getting me a return that I'm happy with. So putting my money in mutual funds is easy for me. I keep some in cash so that I know I can pay for that big credit card bill when I go on vacation. But basically that's it."

Evan may think he's got a winning strategy. He's working hard, enjoying life, investing a little, and keeping up his cash reserves in a way that doesn't stress him out. But he could be making huge financial mistakes without even realizing it. Mutual funds can be a smart piece of anyone's investment mix, but they are rarely the only piece in a wise financial plan.

Here are a handful of questions I would ask Evan. The answers can have a huge impact on his life and his finances.

- You say you're putting away some money, but how do you know you're saving enough for retirement?
- Do you have enough insurance?
- How do you know if the mutual funds you're buying are generating the best returns? Are your funds diversified? What if

> there are other funds with the same fees and risk level that are better for you?
>
> - Do you want to pay more than your fair share in taxes?
> - Will your family be OK if you die, get sued, lose your job, or get sick?
> - Will your money, property, and other assets go quickly where you want them to go if you die or become incapacitated?

As life gets more complicated, an advisor can offer Evan and others like him the following:

- **Peace of Mind**—The confidence of knowing you have a plan to achieve your goals.
- **Accountability**—A resource who will hold you responsible for implementing your financial plan.
- **A Savings Target**—Ensure that you are saving enough today to achieve your goals and maintain your lifestyle in retirement.
- **Tax and Money Savings**—Guidance for how to take advantage of tax breaks, avoid inappropriate or excessive insurance, and invest in a tax-efficient, low-cost, risk-appropriate manner.
- **Fast-Track Goal Achievement**—Reach your goals faster by ensuring that you're not wasting money on overpriced or unnecessary financial products, and that your investments are growing in the most efficient way possible.

■ ■ ■ ■

The Accidental Do-It-Yourselfer

During the Great Recession of 2008 and early 2009, I had a client who had neither the interest nor the time to devote to the management of his family's financial affairs. He is smart and financially savvy, holding an MBA from one of the top-ranked business schools in the United States. The client worked in the corporate finance department of a Fortune 500 company. As he was responsible for making short-term economic forecasts for his employer, he had a hard time de-linking his short-term, extremely negative forecasts from the long-term focus needed for his investment portfolio during the tough economic environment. He was only 50 and wanted to stop working at 55, meaning he could be looking at a good 40 years in retirement.

The client sent me weekly emails to explain the three- to nine-month economic forecasts he was making for his company. He was eager to preserve his wealth, so keeping him invested took a lot of education—and conversation—on my part. Ultimately, he was not able to delegate when the investment waters got too rough, and he sold his holdings near the bottom of the bear market. Sadly, he missed the big returns that the stock market saw in 2009 and subsequent years. The bottom line is that like many proponents of passive investing, I believe stock prices already reflect all available information. Additionally, no one can consistently time the market.

This accidental DIYer learned his lesson the hard way.

Returns of DIY Investors

Every year, DALBAR conducts research to assess how well the average investor did versus the benchmark. Sadly, the average investor's return in some cases didn't beat inflation, which averaged 2.5% annualized between 1990 and 2011.

The "Annualized Investor Returns Versus Benchmarks" chart (Figure 5) provides a good snapshot of the disappointing performance individual investors experience. From 1990 to 2011, the average investor saw an astoundingly low 3.49% annualized return. Over that same time frame, the S&P 500 returned 7.81%.[40] Many bond investors realized similar underperformance: the average bond investor earned 0.9%, while the bond index earned 6.5% annualized over more than two decades. For the 21-year period ending December 31, 2011, both equity and fixed income mutual fund investors underperformed the market for every time frame.[41] This situation was likely due to investors trying to time the market. If you managed your own portfolio, it's likely you did much worse than if you just bought the index and held on for the long term.

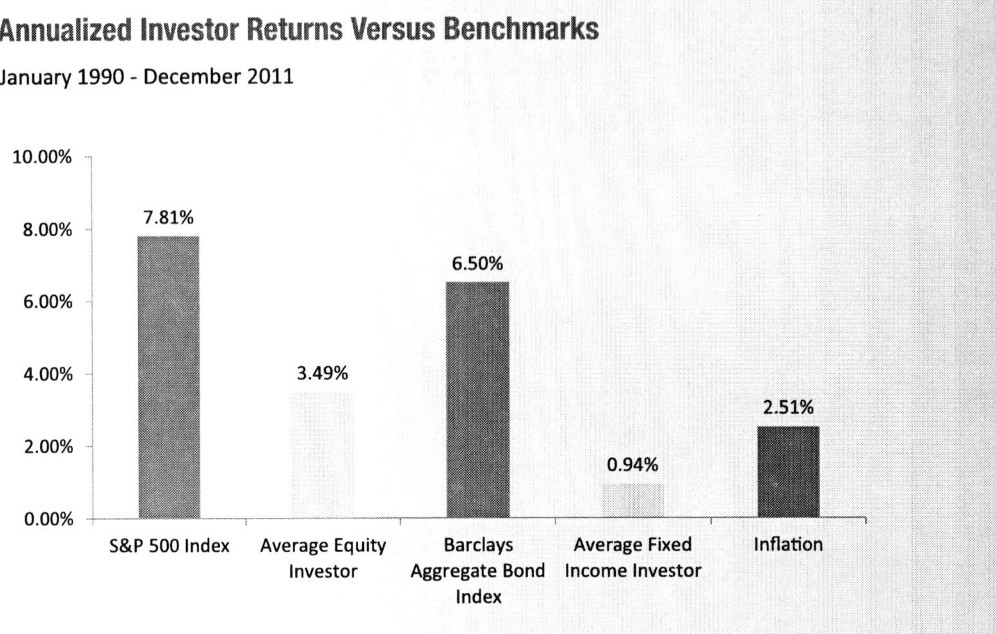

Figure 5. Annualized investor returns versus benchmarks for the 21-year period ending December 31, 2011.[42]

New research from Morningstar shows that compared to a DIY investor, the added value of financial planning can be an extra 1.82% per year to investment returns. Morningstar quantified how much additional retirement income investors can generate by making better financial planning decisions, a measurement Morningstar calls "Gamma." In addition to picking good investments, "good financial-planning decisions are very important to success," says David Blanchett, the head of retirement research for Morningstar Investment Management.[43] "It's hard to quantify the benefit someone receives from a good financial advisor. Gamma is the idea that there is more to just helping someone than picking good funds."

As a CPA who has helped hundreds of people in startups and high-tech companies create plans with their stock options, former Oracle CFO Roy Bukstein believes people who use a third-party advisor to handle their financial affairs have a success rate of 8 on a scale of 1 to 10, with 10 being the most successful. But he gives do-it-yourselfers only a 5 for effectiveness. He cautions people to take a "long-term view. You can't look at it as a short-term [event]. It's a marathon, so choose [your advisor] wisely," says Bukstein.

Consider your own responses to these questions: Where do you get your important information? Do you get it from the media or directly from experts? "What you read in a publication is either static, or historic," says one source. "There's very little projecting the future, [because it] is very hard to do. [Media outlets] always look backwards and it's always [at] the negative stuff. And [the major TV networks are] narrow-minded, not global. When we get our news, we don't have the big picture."[44]

Why Hire a Financial Advisor

Many executives who reflect upon their interests and understand their short-comings early on can get the right help by outsourcing to an advisor who possesses the skills or time they lack. By Phase 3, you already know how to play great offense: you successfully managed risk and parlayed it into real wealth. Now is the time to implement a great defense in order to make your wealth last.

The great defense that an advisor offers is to help you avoid too much risk while guiding you to accept what risk you need to stay ahead of inflation, making sure you're saving enough for the future, ensuring that you have adequate asset protection, giving you clear direction, and identifying any gaps that may exist in your plan. The special value an advisor provides is not telling you the 10 best mutual funds; it's preventing you from making mistakes with your wealth, such as bailing out of the market in the depths of the 2008/2009 Great Recession. Following the recommendations of a smart, ethical advisor will help you save your financial life by making sure you don't make big—but sadly, common—mistakes.

GUIDANCE FROM YOUR PERSONAL CFO

Ideally, your financial planning partner will advise you on more than just investments. Your planner should understand your goals (and review them at every meeting), analyze the resources available to achieve those goals, implement and monitor your asset allocation, and provide specific, actionable instructions for issues outside of his/her direct management. For example, a wise planner can recommend a specific amount of life insurance and offer guidance on asset protection and tax minimization. He or she should provide referrals to professionals to assist you in completing the recommendations.

As your personal financial manager, a planner sees your complete picture. Are you taking unnecessary financial risks? Do you have protection from creditors and others who may try to tap the hard-earned wealth you've worked so hard to build and protect? (The solution to that particular issue could be umbrella liability insurance.) A planner should ask good questions and have meaningful conversations to better understand what's important to you.

Ultimately, outsourcing the management of your personal finances brings you a level of technical competence and expertise about financial management that's similar to what you bring to your career or company. Your advisor should be an extra set of eyes on this important piece of your life; working with a professional forces you to attend to financial affairs. And of course, what you focus on grows.

CAN YOU DIVERSIFY BY ADVISOR?

Some people falsely believe diversification means spreading your assets among several advisors or institutions. While this tactic seems safe, you may actually be doubling up on the same holdings, or buying expensive investments where a lower-cost alternative (often with higher returns) exists. In fact, multiple accounts at different custodians add costs and potential tax inefficiencies that hinder growth, and having assets at many companies could lead to a nightmare for your heirs in the event of your premature death.

OUTSOURCING FINANCIAL MANAGEMENT

Hiring an advisor is a really big step that requires a great deal of research and forethought. Not only must you be confident in the advisor's expertise, knowledge, and follow-through, but you also need to be able to connect and communicate with this person.

Marc Tarpenning, a serial entrepreneur who now acts as a consultant to startups while waiting for his next big thing to come along, says, "Over the years as these liquidity events have happened, frequently I end up thinking, 'Well, what am I going to do with this money?'" He chooses to outsource to a professional to manage it. "As much as I love economics, and I love the micro-picture, I don't get that much out of the minutiae." Tarpenning adds, "I want them to not lose money. I want to just sit there on autopilot and [have my advisor] keep everything going along so that I can do the things that I want to do. I don't want a lot of interaction with them. As long as things are rocking along," he's happy. And when it's time to fund an angel investment or his own company, "I just want the money to be available. I want to be able to say, I'm going to need $100,000 in the next week, because we're going to make an investment."

Many entrepreneurs get big checks every once in a while. Then, there are long periods when no cash comes in. With one of his big checks, Tarpenning carved out a chunk to put into 529s (tax-free college savings plans) for his three children, so "at least I know that college is not going to bankrupt us."

Others outsource their wealth planning to free up time for what they love.. For many entrepreneurs and executives profiled in this book, what they love is not managing their finances, but building companies and spending time with their family.

Focus on Building a Business

Jeff Russakow, who holds a PhD in Mechanical Engineering from Stanford, explained his attitude toward his own personal finances like this: "I know my personality well enough to know I can run and grow a multibillion-dollar business—I love building the valuation of a company—but I don't like managing money. I don't have the discipline to look at my portfolio holdings every day."[45] In addition to discipline, he believes that being a successful investor requires an objectivity that is hard for an entrepreneur or operator to maintain.[46] "If you're someone who builds businesses, you tend to join a team. You're on a mission for years and you have a goal to move one stock. So you genetically and emotionally don't have the discipline to be a great investor, because that's just not how you operate. You do not have good discipline around when to sell. You tend to hold things too long."

As a team-focused company cheerleader in Phases 1 and 2, Russakow says, "You get excited about your company, you focus on your job 110%, and you don't even look at your [company's] market valuation for months at a crack." At that point, "Most of your wealth is usually on paper that you can't liquidate yet. So you're not worried about managing that wealth, just maximizing the value of your company." After the liquidity event, "Suddenly the money shows up and you're like, well I don't really know what to do with it. I'm not very good at actively managing wealth and don't have a passion or discipline for it. I have little experience as an investor. And I am on to my next exciting job or company." He acknowledges that the best way to achieve his goals is to turn over the day-to-day management of his portfolio to "somebody who is going to actively manage it for me who understands" how financial markets operate and what his family's goals are.

Most executives post-liquidity know they should invest their windfall in a diversified portfolio. However, as Russakow explains, "The issue is they don't actually do it. It's not a priority. They put more time into their next project." His advice? "Decide on an investment strategy. Then, find the time or the person to execute on it well."

> One engineer who has had multiple successful liquidity events told me the following: "Through the years, I have certainly had employees who have gotten themselves into trouble by exercising options [and holding the company stock], not thinking through when they were going to have to pay taxes. Entrepreneurs aren't thought of as conservative. But when it comes to [financial] planning, I have always solicited advice and have understood what was going on."[47]

Even VC Lara Druyan, a former investment banker, outsources part of her financial management. This fact surprises her friends and colleagues who say, "You know so much. How come you're not doing it all yourself?"

Her reply? "Because I work and I have children." Smartly, she acknowledges that "unless you're going to devote a significant time and you really know what you're doing, [not outsourcing is] kind of nutty. Because the reason I have someone watching over some of the stuff for me is I just don't have the time." She knows holding on to what she has is about effectively managing it. "People really get fleeced," if they don't protect their hard-earned wealth.

Financial Tune-Ups

Tech workers in a startup often put in 20 hours a day, and several I interviewed told me they did not have time or interest to focus on their personal finances. In a way, that's a good thing, because after a liquidity event, managing your own portfolio without a written plan could put your windfall at risk. On the other hand, some of my sources are DIYers who believe they have the time, temperament, interest, and cautious (but not too cautious) nature to tackle their finances alone.

If, after reading *The Investment Answer* decisions earlier in this chapter—or uncovering your skills, preferences, and weaknesses in other ways—you decide that you are a do-it-yourself investor, consider meeting once a year with an advisor for a tune-up. Find a financial planner who works on an hourly basis, someone you can see as much or as little as you need, possibly only a few hours a year. The planner can review your situation—over and above investments— and provide recommendations for you to act on.

However, if you've decided to outsource to an advisor, consult my guide to finding the right financial planner for you on page 160.

FINANCIAL PLANNING AND TAX TIPS

TIP 10   Rational Diversification Using a 10b5-1 Plan

Sales of stock by certain individuals within any publicly traded company are reported in SEC filings and available to the public. Likewise, blackout periods apply to company insiders and often make selling difficult. However, protecting the assets you worked so hard to amass requires getting out of a concentrated position.

Many financial and legal folks interviewed for this book mentioned the benefits of having a 10b5-1 plan in place. These plans are designed for executives—although employees may also use them—to exercise or sell company stock without being subject to insider trading rules or blackout windows. Number of shares to be traded, share price, and dates are the triggers used for trading company stock under a 10b5-1 plan. Most importantly, a plan can be tailored to the specific needs of the individual who sets it up.[48]

A white paper from Silicon Valley law firm Morrison & Foerster explains the rule this way:

A Rule 10b5-1 plan is a written plan for trading securities that is designed in accordance with Rule 10b5-1(c). Any person executing pre-planned transactions pursuant to a Rule 10b5-1 plan that was established in good faith at a time when that person was unaware of material non-public information has an affirmative defense against accusations of insider trading, even if actual trades made pursuant to the plan are executed at a time when the individual may be aware of material, non-public information that would otherwise subject that person to liability under Section 10(b) of the Exchange Act or Rule 10b5-1. Accordingly, Rule 10b5-1 plans are especially useful for people presumed to have inside information, such as officers and directors.[49]

"I tend to sell over time now," said Yahoo CFO Ken Goldman, a 30-year high-tech veteran. "I use a 10b5 over time, because I don't have the ability to game it. It's just easier as a CFO to use a 10b5 than try to figure out open windows. I think there's a certain group of people that want to hold on and ride it out because they believe so strongly. Financial advisors would tell you to take some money off the table, just average it out, and manage it over time, which I tend to agree with."

Averaging the sales out over time, in a methodical way, gives you a higher chance of capturing the wealth you've created. "You're always ticked off when you think you sell too early, you're ticked off if you think you sell too late," rationalizes Goldman. "There's always seller's remorse."

When asked about the experiences that allow people to hold on to their net worth after an IPO, Goldman offered the following advice:

- "If you already have plenty—more than you ever thought you needed or will need—then it's easier to play it for the long term.
- "If you have pressing debts to repay or commitments to certain things you want to buy right away, you tend to get forced to sell some earlier.
- "If you're in a position where you're totally well-off, then the only question is when to take some off the table, so you don't look stupid in case the stock does go down. But on the other hand, you can ride it [if you] believe the company will do very well, and you'll participate in that. And if it doesn't work perfectly, at least you still feel confident you already have enough net worth that [your personal balance sheet] is not going to be negative."

Kate, a startup executive and attorney profiled in Phase 1, says this about one of her early jobs before 10b5-1 plans became available: "In one of the companies, I was constantly locked up because I always knew that material events were occurring and was unable to sell my shares. [Other] people made millions and millions during that time. If I could have, I would have diversified." Her advice to anyone working at a publicly traded company is to "have a 10b5 plan in place so that as soon as you get the shares, you sell them. Don't hold them." An auto-sell strategy means, "you're really maximizing your value."

As a veteran of multiple high-profile liquidity events, Kate advises employees to "have a 10b5-1 plan in place so that you can devise a plan to sell the shares at certain times or at certain prices. For Employee Stock Purchase Plan (ESPP) shares, I advise selling the shares pursuant to the 10b5-1 plan as soon as you receive them." Automatically selling shares means you're maximizing your personal piece of the value you've created for your company. This plan is especially valuable when you have the chance to buy stock through an employee stock purchase plan. Kate says, "Be sure you have a 10b5-1 plan in place so that as you get the shares, you sell them. Doing so enables you to lock in the 15% or more of value that you receive while not subjecting the stock to market risk."

A 10b5-1 plan is great for the company, too. One employee of a hot tech company who didn't have a 10b5-1 plan told me that during the first six months after the IPO, she checked the stock price—hourly—to figure out the best time to sell. That came at the company's expense. When she was checking the stock price, she wasn't focused on her work. I heard this story over and over from sources involved in IPOs.

A Rule 10b5-1 plan is generally set up by a law firm or your company using a template. The plan is a contract between the broker, the company, and the employee. To avoid any appearance of insider trading, it's best not to make modifications, terminations, or suspensions to a plan. Therefore, set up your personal plan only after thoughtful consideration of your individual situation during the plan's time horizon—likely for years, or until you leave the company.

TIP 11 Dollar Cost Averaging

Dollar cost averaging (DCA) is a strategy used to invest slowly in your portfolio, rather than investing everything at once. A three-, six-, nine-, 12-, or 18-month DCA is usually appropriate when you're investing a large portion of your assets in the market; for example, if you sell your company stock, which was the majority of your net worth. Or if you received an inheritance. A DCA is also reasonable if you are concerned about investing at the top of the market (yet no one has a crystal ball, so no one knows in advance where the top of the market is). If you have a very long time horizon—at least 10 to 15 years—until the funds are needed, it's very likely the market will be higher in 10 years than it is today, even if it goes down for some period of time in the interim.

A downside to dollar cost averaging is that trading fees may be increased. Investing the entire amount at once means you pay trading fees only once.

TIP 12   Mortgages for Buying and Remodeling a Home

Generally, you can deduct all of the interest you pay on a home mortgage, up to $1.1 million, as long as the funds were used to buy, build, or maintain your primary or second home. If you already own a home that you wish to remodel, a home equity line of credit (HELOC) may be used to pay for your remodel. The interest on the HELOC is 100% deductible, as long as the HELOC and primary mortgage together don't total more than $1.1 million, and the loans were used to buy, build, or maintain the property. Any interest paid on the portion of the loans over $1.1 million is not tax deductible. Beware that if you pay cash for the remodel (or for a home for that matter), you can't later take out a loan and deduct the interest, since "non-acquisition indebtedness" is not tax deductible.

TIP 13   Tax Loss Harvesting

Harvesting losses is a brilliant wealth-creating technique. Selling your loss positions is a sure way to offset gains realized during the year and stockpile losses for future years. Capital losses in excess of capital gains can reduce other income by $3,000; any excess loss is carried forward for use in a future year. Remember that if you sell stock for less than you paid for it, the wash sale rules bar deducting a loss on a security when a virtually identical one is purchased within 30 days of the sale. Long-term investors can retain exposure to their chosen portfolio by purchasing a similar holding after selling the loss position. When the stock market is volatile, it is a great time to harvest losses. In times when the stock market is rising, mutual funds often distribute large capital gains that would be offset by capital losses. If enough losses are harvested in your account during a market correction, you'll see the benefit for many years to come in the form of lower annual tax bills. (For an example of how this technique is used in practice, see the story of my husband's liquidity event in the preface.)

TIP 14 Tax Rates

Understanding a few definitions can help lower your tax bill.

> **Capital gain** is the tax treatment for the sale of a capital asset, such as company stock or mutual funds. Long-term capital gains on assets held for more than one year are currently taxed at rates much lower than wages.

> **Ordinary income** is taxed at your marginal income tax bracket. The more wage, bonus, and equity award income you earn, the higher your tax bracket. Tax rates are tiered; once you hit the highest tax bracket, any future ordinary income is taxed at the top income tax rate. There is an exception for alternative minimum tax, which is an additional tax applied on top of your regular tax, often at a rate below your marginal tax bracket.

TIP 15 Investment Time Horizon

Investing by definition means to take on risk. Markets are volatile, but over long periods of time produce returns higher than inflation.

In the following two charts, you can see the performance of five asset classes over an 86-year time horizon: U.S. Treasury bills (cash), long-term bonds, corporate bonds, large-cap stocks, and small-cap stocks. Comparing the performance of one-year returns versus 25-year rolling returns, you can get a good picture of the volatility and long-term performance of each asset class.

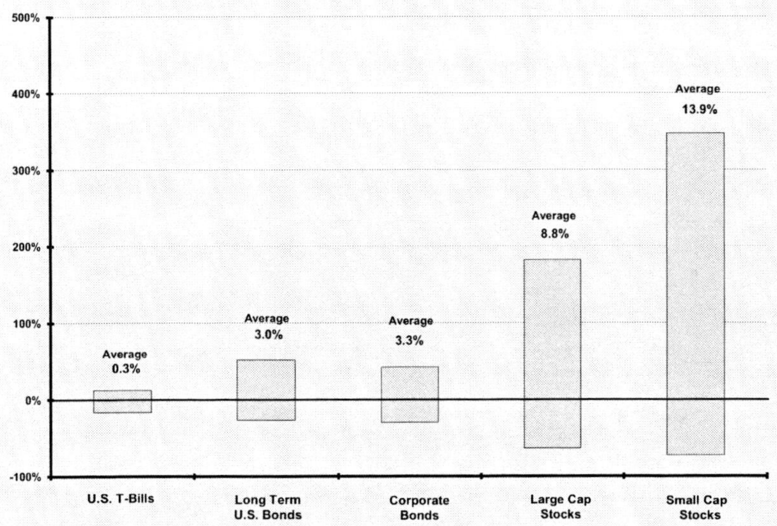

Figure 6. Inflation-adjusted returns for one-year holding periods from 1926 to 2013.[50]

In the one-year holding period chart, each asset class has seen both positive and negative returns. Even cash and bonds failed to preserve principal during periods of high inflation. Looking to the right side of this chart, large- and small-cap stocks are clearly the most volatile in the short term.

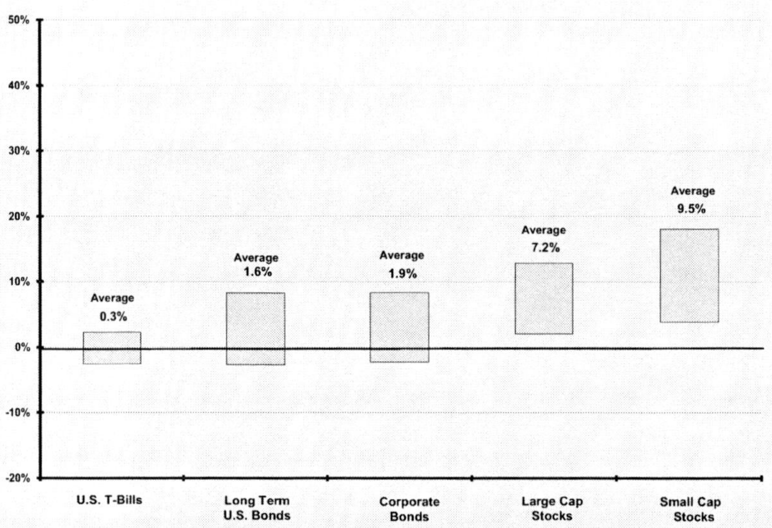

Figure 7. Inflation-adjusted returns for 25-year holding periods from 1926 to 2013.[51]

In each 25-year holding period, large- and small-cap stocks have never had negative returns. This may seem counterintuitive, but it makes sense: you're paid more to hold riskier assets, and over time, returns converge on long-term historical performance. Therefore, it's important to hold cash in the short term, and invest in a diversified equity portfolio for the long term.

A financial planning partner can help you avoid the emotional pitfalls involved in concentration and diversification, adjust investment plans to a comfortable level of risk for you, and have meaningful conversations to better understand what's important to you.

Checklist for Startup Employees in Phase 3

FOR EVERYONE WORKING IN THE STARTUP:

- ❏ If applicable, begin to diversify your concentrated stock position, using a decision tree analysis if desired.

- ❏ Sign up for the 10b5-1 plan, to sell your stock on an ongoing basis, regardless of blackout windows.

- ❏ Create a financial plan with the help of a financial planner (or do it yourself). Identify your short- and long-term goals. Perform analyses on your assets and understand potential tax implications, and divide your wealth into buckets: Maintain, Risk, and Give.

- ❏ Create and implement an investment plan. Understand your short- and long-term risk tolerance.

- ❏ Hold a family meeting to determine goals for your family (or if you are single, check in with yourself).

- ❏ Consider whether charitable giving is important to you. If so, start to create and execute a charitable giving strategy.

- ❏ Update or create estate planning documents incorporating your goals and values. Set up a trust to protect your privacy and other estate planning documents to carry out your wishes.

- ❏ As family challenges come up, take advantage of employee assistance programs that your company may provide.

- ❏ If you're a DIYer, you'll get no value from an unimplemented plan. So be sure to make the time to plow through all your action items and meet any deadlines.

PHASE 4
WHAT'S NEXT?

Post-Transition Phase
2–40 Years

The Four Phases of Startup Life[SM]

	Phase 1	Phase 2	Liquidity Event	Phase 3	Phase 4
	Pre-Transition 2-40 years **Laying the Foundation**	**Pre-Transition** 0-24 months **Ramping Up**		**Post-Transition** 1-24 months **Realizing the Dream**	**Into the Future** 2-40 years **What's Next?**
Quality of Life Challenges					
	Preoccupation with startup Loneliness Optimism Tenacity	Maintaining balance while working long hours Excitement Persistence		Weighing career options If you stay: Vest in peace and maintain work-life balance If you leave: Figure out what's next	Flexibility and choices Charitable activities Travel New career or startup Passion projects
Financial Challenges					
	Raising capital Below-market salary Accountability to investors Funnel all resources to create and build the company	Increasing enterprise value Salary and bonus Accountability to investors, management, and board Planning with equity awards		Increasing enterprise value and stock price Accountability to shareholders, board, and management Diversification of concentrated position Expensive purchases	New or second home Venture or angel investing Strategizing goals with financial resources

Common to All Phases

Challenge	Maximize Value of Equity Awards (ISO, NQ, RSA, RSU, ESPP)
Concerns	Wealth Preservation Tax Reduction Wealth Protection Passing Assets to Heirs Charitable Giving
Solutions	Personal CFO Expert Team of Advisors Financial Education

WHAT'S NEXT?

THE "WHAT'S NEXT?" PHASE BRINGS at least a short break from work for most people, during which they can explore their passions before retiring or going on to their next project. Several paths exist in Phase 4, depending on your situation.

IF YOU ARE INDEPENDENTLY WEALTHY

You have many choices. Read about the BE WISE Planning Strategy in the appendix to learn how to tap into your passions if you plan on retiring. If you don't wish to stop working, you'll want to get back to work soon or you may have to make up for lost time. Either way, protect your wealth, so you can stop working when you'd like to slow down.

IF YOU REALIZED A LARGE LIQUIDITY EVENT, BUT CAN'T AFFORD TO STOP WORKING

You may take time off to travel or spend with your family—but beware of staying out too long. The maximum time off, if you want to eventually get back in the game, is six months to two years, because both technology and influential people change quickly.

IF YOU ARE AN ENTREPRENEUR

For the true entrepreneur, it's back to Phase 1 as soon as possible, regardless of wealth. See my book for entrepreneurs, *Startup Wealth*, where you'll find the

Entrepreneur's Wheel of Life, easy-to-follow checklists, and crucial planning tips to help you achieve financial success from your startup and avoid making fatal financial errors.

> "When you're finished changing, you're finished."
> —Benjamin Franklin

From my research and interviews for this book—and many more casual conversations—it's clear that Phase 4 means vastly different things to different people. Free of contractual ties, and after full vesting of pre-IPO options or stock, Phase 4 gives executives and employees a delightful opportunity to explore.

With newfound financial flexibility, Phase 4 can last anywhere from two to 40 years. Financial independence for younger people (generally, under age 40) means you are likely to go to another startup or get involved in a passion project, such as a charitable cause. Many mid-career or older executives use this opportunity to realize their dreams and follow pursuits unrelated to work in a company, such as charitable giving, travel, and spending time with family. Some continue to work into their 60s and beyond.

Those who received a bump in wealth but can't yet stop working often go to another startup. Fewer folks stay at the current iteration of the startup, now a larger and more formal company. Others do consulting work in which the hours are less intense.

Avoid Traps for the Unwary in Phase 4

If you're financially independent, Phase 4 is the time when you get to do what makes you happy without the pressure of bringing home the bacon. It's dangerous to enter Phase 4 without a plan; unless you create activities to fill your days, you can become depressed and feel unfulfilled. Some people experience a sense of loss after their liquidity event. Others feel guilty. They may apologize for not working or feel discomfort for the fortune that's put them in a different financial league than their friends or family. "I've definitely seen guilt over feeling like they're not somehow doing enough," says one Silicon Valley–based VC.[1]

USING GOOD FORTUNE TO ENJOY LIFE: DAVE BUCHANAN

MARKETING EXECUTIVE AT EXTREME NETWORKS DURING ITS 1999 IPO.[2]

"Dave is enjoying life in Berkeley." That's how I was introduced to him.

Dave Buchanan has worked in an incredible variety of roles, including engineer, product manager, and manager of Asian markets for companies ranging from behemoths like Sun and HP to a number of early-stage startups.

From the late 1970s to the early 2000s, he experienced the Silicon Valley high-tech community from a unique vantage point. He literally made the rounds in the Valley. When he started at Sun, he told the orientation leader, "Don't worry, I know where the bathrooms are. I worked in this building a year and a half ago for a different company." That same campus is now home to Facebook.

Buchanan achieved moderate success at the companies he worked for. Yet his lucky break came only toward the end of his 30-year career, when his best friend asked him to join Extreme Networks, "a feisty little startup," says Buchanan, who was the first non-engineer hired.

Nimble Startups Allow for Quick Decisions

Buchanan really enjoyed making decisions on the fly in the early days at Extreme. As the business development manager, he received a phone call one day from a university purchasing agent. "What's your university discount program?" the caller asked.

"Hold on one second," said Buchanan. He ran over to the next cube belonging to the VP of Sales, who had just been hired the week before. Quickly explaining the situation, Buchanan asked, "What should we do for him?"

"Thirty-five percent?" asked the new VP.

"'Yeah, that sounds good. That'll be our program.' So I pick up the phone and say, 'We have a university discount program. It's 35%,'" remembers Buchanan.

Soon after, negotiating for the company's first OEM (original equipment manufacturing) deal, he advised the co-founder/CEO to ask for a minimum sales guarantee in the contract, pushing the envelope a bit. The founder's response was "Do you think they'd do that?" Buchanan had calculated the guarantee to be a very small part of the buyer's overall revenue, while for Extreme, the $5 million sale was "our whole business plan for the first year. We asked for it and they didn't blink an eye." At the Christmas party a few days later, the CEO announced they were doubling the first-year sales goal from $5 to $10 million. "It was pretty clear we were onwards and upwards, just like that," says an excited Buchanan.

Enjoying Life

As a result of the Extreme Networks IPO, Buchanan achieved financial independence.

He agrees that luck plays a huge part in business success. After working at a handful of startups early in his career, "I realized it was a dice roll, and the dice is loaded against you, so you're going to have to roll it a number of times before you're going to hit it on a startup," acknowledges Buchanan. After the Extreme Networks IPO, Buchanan stayed just long enough—exactly four years from his hire date. "Not coincidentally, because you know how these stock options work." Buchanan laughs, "I vested out, and boom, I was out of there.

"There are a certain number of chairs in the Valley: several hundred of them had 'VP of Marketing' on them, and it was a game of musical chairs. That number of chairs was shrinking pretty precipitously every year," Buchanan says about the consolidation that was happening at the turn of the century, when he was planning his next career move. "I had to ask myself, 'Do I really want to fight for one of those chairs?' Financially, I don't really need it. I'm taking it away from someone who probably needs it more." And just like that, he stopped all pursuit of full-time work.

Besides, Buchanan's passions lie elsewhere. His view of enjoying life means spending time with family, including his two daughters and his mom, working with his hands on residential home construction projects, and making music. In his late teens, Buchanan supported himself as a full-time rock musician in Chicago. After his success at Extreme, he reunited his band and flew the members out to California to record a CD. His family members were involved, too—including his mom, who sang a cappella to German Christmas carols—and everyone had a great time.

Judiciously Investing His Wealth

As for his personal finances, Buchanan outsources this part of his life to professionals. A former colleague manages the bulk of his nest egg. Buchanan also has real estate investments with another friend. During the early days of a startup, "it's all about really focusing your resources and your attention on this one thing to make it happen. That's not how you want to invest later," he cautions. "To preserve wealth, you want to diversify. You're not just [investing in] this one thing." The best route would be to realize you've been very lucky, and to create a plan to preserve your wealth.

■ ■ ■ ■

Finding a Place in the World Outside of Work

For 25 years, a Bay Area high-tech investor had mini liquidity events.[3] In early 2008, unable to find good companies at a good value to invest in, he decided to step off the fast track. He knew he could afford to never work again. "I sit on a lot of boards, chair a couple of boards, and I do some private investing of my own money. But I don't have a thing, a single thing that I do," the 49-year-old financial wiz says. "When I left my company, I had this expectation that a couple of years later I would find the new thing. But the new thing wasn't obvious," he recalls. "I'm trying to find the right thing to jump into and I can't find it." He wonders if his current struggle is because for all his working life, he set the bar really high for himself. "It is hard when you're 40-something years old to find a passion that may not have been simmering in there along the way."

He acknowledges that it would have been easier to figure out the "What's next?" of his Phase 4 if he had thought more about his passions in Phases 1 and 2. "It's hard to develop passions" after you've devoted all of your time for two decades to work and family.

On the day he retired, he had no hobbies. So he tried to find some. "I always really wanted to be a great golfer. And I played once in a while, but now I'm going to go really pour myself into it." The only problem? He doesn't really like golf.

He wishes he had done some heavy reflecting and soul searching about his personal happiness earlier. He advises other executives to consider carving out time "when you're on an airplane," for example, to ask, "'If I had more time, what would I really want to do?'" What he didn't realize in his 20s and 30s was, "there's a life [outside of work]. You're not going to do this for your entire life." However, he cautions, "There is an advantage to having some idea, but I'm not sure you want to have it completely mapped out." After telling me about his new office, I asked him what he does there, and he laughed. "I get away from my house."

He continues to experiment with his newfound daytime freedom. One of the projects he has found and is most proud of is creating college scholarships for low-income students, since he is passionate about education.

Having the ability to stop working seems glamorous. Yet when it happens suddenly, it can be a shock. The investor explains that once he had more wealth than he needed, his job became making meaningful decisions to impact his life. In Phase 2, working in a pre-transition company leading up to the liquidity event, you may have worked insanely long hours to get your company sold or taken public. "And then boom, it happens," he says. Now you don't have to work on the weekends. The reality of this hit him only after he was already there: "Whoa, what am I going to do?" he remembers.

He dubs this period "rejoining your family."

Like many executives, his family did their own thing when he was still working. "I used to get up early to go to work, and I wouldn't see my kids in the morning," remembers the investor. "And now, I'm there in the morning when the kids are getting ready for school. And it felt like I was rejoining a party that was already happening." His wife had figured out a system for getting the kids to school in the morning that didn't include him. At one point, she told him to leave, saying, "We're on a schedule." He concludes, "It's awkward figuring out how you rejoin your own family."

The takeaway is to get to know yourself and what you enjoy. Otherwise, you could end up unfulfilled when your work commitments stop.

A PURPOSE BEYOND MONEY

One hard-charging CEO on his fourth company told me the story of a billionaire friend who custom-built a $20 million house on a golf course.[4] He invited 10 couples over to his new house for a party, ranging in age from 50 to 62.[5] The guys were in the billiard room, and the women were somewhere else. Of these 10 guys, half were still working, half weren't. The wealthiest guy was probably working the hardest. The five who weren't working were playing golf five days a week and told the working men how crazy they were for continuing to work.

As the conversation progressed, there was a transformation between the two groups. At first, the guys who were working hard were thinking, "Maybe I shouldn't work this hard." And then, by the end of the conversation, the guys who were working hard were feeling sorry for the guys not working, "because they had very little purpose in their lives," said the CEO. "Particularly early on, we're in business to accumulate the wealth necessary to have the quality of life [we desire]. Once we have the wealth, there should be a reassessment. In reality, you should design your life early on to have quality of life from the beginning. Very seldom are people happy if they don't have some purpose beyond golf."[6]

The challenge, after selling your company or being part of a successful wealth event, is avoiding boredom. At his first company, the CEO remembers, "I had four assistants out in front of my office, and I was flying around North America on a private jet. Then, all of a sudden I'm home and my wife won't even go out to lunch with me. There's nothing to do. You're trying to figure out, 'What do I do now?'"

Technology entrepreneurs are like movie stars. Deal lawyer Mark Cameron White says, "You read in the press that actors are always concerned about their next job. They're making a gazillion dollars, they don't have to work, but their self-worth is defined by their role in their next movie." Encouraging reflection, he asks, "What is the currency you have in life? You've got money, you've got reputation, and then you've got respect. Reputation is your legacy. It's what you're known for. It's your contribution that you've done in the past. But respect is what you are doing now. Are you a has-been or are you a player?"

Stories like these can make retiring a scary thought.

TIME OFF BETWEEN COMPANIES

If you plan to return to work after taking a break, be careful that you're not gone for too long.

"The topline issue is, how long are you going to be absent before you get back into the game again?" asks White, who works closely with serial entrepreneurs who are building their companies.

After a liquidity event, many people take time off, if only to find the next venture or job. You've used so much mental and physical energy taking a company to a successful exit. While it's exhilarating, it's also exhausting. You may not have to get up in the morning and work right away, but the length of your break depends on the size of the exit and how you define success.

It's tricky, says White, "because your skill set becomes pretty antiquated really fast in this community. I can't speak about Kansas, but here, if you're out of it for six months, the world changes. The folks that are important change, the sectors that are emerging and becoming more interesting change, relationships get stale." He remembers clients who "have not been active for a year, and it's harder for them to get back involved and figure out what's going on; you're not embraced because you're yesterday's history."

White offers a time-off timeline. "The younger you are, the transition period is shorter. The older you are, the transition period is longer. If you're in your 50s, it's 24 months. If you're in your 40s, it's 12 months. If you are in your 30s, it's three to six months. Is it linear? No. But in broad parameters, probably yes. The reason is, it's not just business. It's also about your family obligations. If you're in your late 30s or early 40s, you've got children that are 5 to 12 years old, so you're going to pay attention to them. In Phase 1, when you built the company, you were not around; you want to make up for lost time [in Phase 4]. But then again, you [take time off] for 12 months, and you're like a fish out of water." You have to balance family and business.

"In today's world, if you're fortunate enough to have your health, what you have in later phases is more flexibility of time," says Yahoo CFO Ken Goldman, a three-time IPO veteran who took both Excite@Home and Fortinet public. You can work with boards and charities, travel, and find more creative ways to spend time. "There's no reason at any age to think about how to stop." Besides, he cautions, "If you drop out, you become irrelevant."

Everyone Needs a Personal Life Plan

One day you're at work all day, and the day after you retire, you have all day to have coffee. That doesn't mentally compute for most people who are healthy, vibrant, and used to long workdays. Some try out different activities after they retire: community involvement, volunteering on boards, mentoring. "What strikes me," confides Richard Pivnicka, a Silicon Valley lawyer, advisor, and Honorary Czech Consul General, "is that everyone who is transitioning into that mode is apprehensive. They don't have a nice plan that they would look forward to. I never met any of these guys who look forward to their new phase in their life more than their past."[7]

The BE WISE Planning Strategy is a concise way to organize your goals and values. The ideal personal life plan would address everything from vacations to volunteer work, board membership to business mentoring—"the whole canopy of things one would do when you don't have to go downtown every day," says Pivnicka, whose eyes were opened to this idea when he stopped working full-time in his early 50s and noticed the butterflies in his backyard for the first time. "It seemed the days were quite long until I put together the game plan of those things I like to do to make life interesting, exciting, and fulfilling," he remembered. He believes his plan would have been even more powerful had he put it in writing.

"It's trepidatious moving into your 'what I always want to do with my life' zone from the day-to-day work. But once you make that leap—if you can do that—it's very, very rewarding," says Pivnicka. "Now, I'm taking fencing lessons, I've built my first seven-foot bronze sculpture, and last week I was in Washington, arguing with the patent office on my first patent." One of his favorite things to do is judge and mentor a business plan competition at the University of Notre Dame. He's very active in the Bay Area tech and business communities, and as an enthusiastic oenophile, he likes to host dinners in his wine cellar. Clearly, Pivnicka is enjoying Phase 4.

PICK UP THE BANJO OR WIN AN ACADEMY AWARD

For inspiration on how to confront the flexibility that accompanies Phase 4, look to Warren Hellman, a private equity pioneer who, after reaching financial independence, returned to his love of the banjo.

After enjoying a successful career, Hellman spent time with his family and fostered his love of music. He lived a full life before his death in 2011 at age 77[8] and will be remembered for accomplishments ranging from prescient investing to major support of charities. A respected philanthropist, Hellman donated generously to a variety of causes in San Francisco: museums, the ballet, a non-profit news organization, a local health clinic, and the public school system. David Lee, the executive director of the Chinese American Voters Education Committee and a commissioner at the San Francisco Recreation and Parks Department, stated, "If this city had a patron, he was it. He's a grandfather figure of San Francisco and a man who cared deeply about the city and had a vision that included everybody, not just the business community."

Hellman's business accomplishments are no less impressive. While his early experience was in finance, he gravitated to the tech world. After working for Lehman Brothers and becoming the firm's youngest president, he started Matrix Partners, a venture capital firm that was an early investor in Apple. Next, he founded Hellman & Friedman, a private equity firm, where one of his well-known deals was the sale of DoubleClick (which Hellman & Friedman owned) to Google.

Another thing Hellman is known for: *SF Weekly* dubbed Hellman one of the best-known "*incidental* banjo players—that is, people who are otherwise well known who also play a mean banjo."[9] Hellman learned to play the banjo in his 20s as an up-and-coming investment banker but gave it up during the bulk of his working years. He returned to the instrument in his late 60s, when he gradually started easing out of his company duties (though he never really left the firm that had his name on the office door). Around the same time, he also created and personally funded what has become probably the "single biggest weekend of free music in America": the Hardly Strictly Bluegrass Festival, which takes place each year in San Francisco's Golden Gate Park in Hellman Hollow (renamed from Speedway Meadows in Hellman's honor shortly before his death). The festival attracts nearly one million listeners with both big and small names in the lineup.

One of those HSB bands, the Wronglers, was Hellman's own. If you had the opportunity to see the group perform, you would have heard what the *Deal* magazine dubs Hellman's "irreverent" lyrics: "Pickers, pluckers, plonkers born, to strum, perchance to croon, drifting through the cosmos, playing out of tune." Music brought Hellman joy and even some fame. He and the Wronglers were asked to perform at the Austin music festival South by Southwest. While he was watching another act, "Some guy comes up and says, 'Hey, aren't you with the Wronglers?' I was an investment banker 40 years and not one person recognized me anywhere . . . I said, 'Man, you just made my life.'" By identifying what he loved, Hellman was able to live out his retirement, sharing his passion for music with others.[10]

Jeff Skoll, the number two in the early days at eBay, is another example of someone who used a liquidity event to pursue a passion.[11] After spending some time at Knight-Ridder in the mid-1990s, where he tried to push the newspaper giant into new media, Skoll joined eBay as its president and first employee. He left two years later—Meg Whitman came in, back problems forced him out of full-time work—and subsequently sold half his stake for a cool $2 billion. Skoll then used that money to start Participant Media, the production company responsible for a string of provocative and award-winning feature and documentary films, including the Oscar winner *An Inconvenient Truth*. "Movies that make a difference," an influential longtime Valley connector notes. "He achieved his goal. He's happy with what he's done, and he exceeded his expectations."[12]

One Silicon Valley executive I spoke with serves as an example of how it's possible to live out your artistic passions without underwriting a music festival or movie production company.[13] After working and volunteering in the Silicon Valley community for decades, the CEO looks forward to using his upcoming retirement to pursue something he is enthusiastic about: art. In our interview, he spoke excitedly of his passion, which started as a way to relieve stress. Focusing his retirement on his art will allow the CEO to stay busy while doing something that makes him happy.

Whether you make music or art, spending money is a personal choice. You will be lucky if, like Hellman, Skoll, and the Silicon Valley CEO, you can find a passion to pursue.

Charitable Giving

After a liquidity event, many people consider giving some of their sizable new wealth to a charitable cause. In the tech community, alma maters are especially popular charity recipients, because "they want to give back to the school that gave to them," reasons CPA Jason Graham.

DONOR-ADVISED FUNDS:

A WEALTH-CREATING STRATEGY FOR CHARITABLE GIVING

Donating appreciated securities, instead of cash, to fund your charitable giving can increase your wealth. It's a great way to mitigate taxes and help your favorite causes.

Graham explains how this works: "Let's say they just had a spike in income of $500,000. So to offset that $500,000, they could give that $500,000 to charity." Often, that's more than they might normally give to charity, and they may be overwhelmed by determining which charity they would give that much to in one year. However, using a donor-advised fund, "they get the deduction today, and they can spread [their gifts to charities] out over a period of time." The logistics are simple: a donor funds a charitable pot that she or he can later draw from. And a lot of young tech executives with some financial success like that idea. To make giving even more efficient, rather than putting cash in that donor-advised fund, Graham advises putting appreciated stock in, because you avoid paying tax on the gain on that appreciated stock. You get to take a tax deduction for the fair market value of that stock, even if your basis was practically nothing, and you're able to avoid the capital gain on that appreciation. (See page 153 explaining donor-advised funds in more detail.)

USING WEALTH TO ADVANCE YOUR PRIORITIES

Partially in response to his concern about how the schools in China are "churning out very high-quality engineers at a rate that's much higher than we are," Tesla Motors founder Martin Eberhard and his wife, Carolyn, established the Eberhard Engineering Scholarship Fund at their alma mater, the University of Illinois. The goal of the scholarship is "to encourage people to be engineers, particularly women," says Eberhard, who has received help from the university to set up and monitor the scholarship. "They choose the person by our rules." This direction is what the Eberhards really like, because "what we're looking for is a creative person," who could one day create companies just like the fund's benefactor has done with Tesla and NuvoMedia.

HOW TO MAKE A MEANINGFUL CHARITABLE IMPACT

Do you want your favorite charity to benefit during your lifetime or after you die? The benefit to giving during your lifetime is that the charity can put your money to work now and acknowledge your generosity. A gift to a charity upon your death is conservative, in that only your "excess" funds—money you don't need to support your lifestyle while you're alive—are donated, ensuring that you never run out. A gift upon death may be done through your trust or will, or by setting up a separate charitable trust.

PROFILE
YAHOO'S CFO: KEN GOLDMAN

YAHOO HAD NEARLY $5 BILLION IN REVENUE IN 2012.[14] CFO OF EXCITE@HOME (IPO IN 1996)[15] AND FORTINET (IPO IN 2009).[16] TOOK BOTH COMPANIES PUBLIC.

Yahoo CFO Ken Goldman is confident, well respected, and successful. I heard him talk at a Wharton CFO Roundtable event in San Francisco in October 2011 and was impressed with his maturity, easy speaking style, and wisdom. His presence on the panel, like most things Goldman does, was just another way he stays connected to the high-tech community. He thrives on being in the center of cutting-edge ideas and was CFO for various companies through four acquisitions

and two IPOs. That night, he arrived late, due to his son's water polo
championship game. He thoughtfully answered the questions from
the moderator. He also doled out some advice, including:

- Have mentors.
- Go where the action is.
- Live in a good neighborhood but avoid owning the nicest house
  on the block.
- Hire smart people from great schools, rather than employees
  from another company you have to train.

"What I work for is both for charities and for my kids," said
Goldman during our interview. "There's not a ton more I'm going to
do personally for myself. How you set your kids up, and how you do
things for charitable purposes more than anything else is how I think
about the accumulation of assets and resources." He continued, "Full-
time work begets working on for-profit boards [and] charitable boards,
because your name is out there and people remember you. Otherwise, you get lost. You find ways to make time for travel and vacation,
including having second homes, [and] pick your leisure choices.

"I've had the same exercise trainer for probably 13 or 14 years,"
Goldman confided. "He did say that I used to drive a Suzuki Samurai,
and then I went to a Mazda 626, and now I have a Porsche. I guess I've
changed a little bit from the time he knew me [in my first company]
in terms of what I have now. Same house, but I have changed cars."
Goldman spent some of his IPO wealth on a second home and new
cars, "but not frou-frou stuff. I don't spend a lot of money on jewelry,
don't spend money on things that I don't find some real value to. And
even second homes, we looked at prices that at least in our opinion
are reasonable.

"The more you do something, the more you know what to do.
Therefore, the more you can leverage your experience, the more you
can delegate certain activities and see things," Goldman advised,
referring to the big picture of running a company. "I use the term
'pattern recognition.' You have so much perspective from having seen

so many things, you're able to be much more effective in your role.

"We have a very entrepreneurial culture out here [in the Bay Area]. A lot of those people who are taking money off the table [cashing out their company stock] early are reinvesting that in new ventures. The other positive is that they're using that to start up their own company," says Goldman. When they don't need to take a salary, "it gives them freedom, which is one of the attributes of this whole geographic area, where people are really driving new startups very, very fast because a lot of people have the wherewithal to do it. They don't need to wait to raise money from angel investors or other venture guys. Or they become angels themselves and they invest in a bunch of other companies. And they get their jollies doing that."

Speaking about his personal assets, Goldman said he's heavily invested in technology. In fact, about one-third of his net worth is in the tech sector. However, in any one pre-IPO company, he'd bet less than 1% of his net worth, and in any individual investment, the maximum he'd invest is less than 3%. When asked if having a third of his net worth in technology is a different investment philosophy than when he was younger, he replied, "Oh yeah. I didn't have a third to give away."

■ ■ ■ ■

Angel Investing: Tips, Motivations & Overconfidence

From my research, it has become apparent that when entrepreneurs, executives, and employees have a big liquidity event, they usually don't stay out of the game for long.

Many stay involved by becoming angel investors or working with accelerators (startup incubators), though the motivations behind this decision can differ. Some like the bragging rights of being involved in the creation of cool technology—and the chance to make money at it. But most just love the excitement of building companies, creating products, and cultivating new ideas, but want to avoid the grueling 16-hour workdays that accompany launching their own startups.

While Peter Herz, an engineer and serial entrepreneur in his early 50s, oscillates between angel investing and entrepreneurial endeavors, he recognizes that "when I get out to my 60s and 70s, the goal is that I have a number of these projects that I can help out in," acknowledging he wants to help as "an advisor or in a board capacity, and keep plugged in but not in the day-to-day management of companies. I enjoy learning about a new business area, new concepts, new issues that companies have" and that's where he wants to spend his time. Angel investing is a way to stay involved in what he loves without the pressures of operating in the daily grind.

For others, like Rob Nail, angel investing simply makes sense, because he likes cool technology, and tech is the business he's been in for the past 10 years. To Stephen Roth, a software development entrepreneur, angel investing can feed the ego and the aspirations of his wallet: "We [as entrepreneurs] can relate to the struggles, and I want to help out. But of course I'm not doing it as a charity case. I'm doing it because I also want to succeed and make money."[17] Finally, some feel invincible after their first success. They did so well with their own company, surely (they assume) if they invest in a promising startup, they'll have another big win.

OPPORTUNITIES ARE EVERYWHERE

"If you've had a liquidity event, most likely you have a network of people you've worked with, people you trust," says venture capitalist Lara Druyan. "The great thing about Silicon Valley is there are always new companies starting up." As a successful entrepreneur or employee, "You end up besieged by opportunities to invest in little companies."

A very attractive reason to be an angel investor is to stay in the game and see what's hot. So even if you're not "employed" full-time by your previous company, or by a new startup, you can continue to practice your craft and stay current, as an investor. "And in Silicon Valley—in technology, in particular— that's a super important thing to do. Because everything's always changing." Other reasons Druyan sees to angel invest? "Because [the founders are] friends of yours, because you're helping and advising, because you're keeping current, or because you may decide that you want to join one of these" companies one day. After people have been successful, they feel like they may have something to impart to other people, including lessons learned, functional expertise, and industry expertise.

Most angel investors want to have an active role of some sort in the company. Thus, angel investing is a way to climb aboard a startup's ship. "It's a way for them to look around, see what's going on, see what they like to do, and if they think it's an opportunity, they hoist themselves in with their first investment and they expand their role over time," says transactional attorney Mark Cameron White.

RISKS IN ANGEL INVESTING

Whatever the reason you might become an angel investor, there are real risks involved. Dr. Scott A. Shane, a Professor of Entrepreneurial Studies at Case Western Reserve University and author of *Fool's Gold: The Truth Behind Angel Investing in America*, explains the low odds of success in an interview with *Failure* magazine.[18] "Less than 0.2% of angel-backed companies end in an IPO, and less than 1.5% end in an acquisition." Shane continues, "Forty percent of the investments return less money than the capital that goes in," while only "Seven percent of the investments account for 75% of all returns. It's the few phenomenal outcomes that make up for the losses of most." He stresses that it's important to be realistic and understand what people typically earn from investing in startups. "If you think the typical angel investment is going to return an internal rate of return of 30% per year, you are going to be very disappointed unless you are really lucky."

START SLOWLY

Optimize your chances of a positive return on your angel investments by doing your research and listening to those who have done it successfully. "My advice would be don't start with an angel investment,"[19] urges Nicolai Wadstrom, CEO and Founder of BootstrapLabs, a business lab and accelerator for European, Asian, and Silicon Valley technology startups located in the San Francisco Bay Area.[20] "It's the first time, so that's when you're going to make all the mistakes. Usually people—myself included—[tend to be] a little bit too sure of themselves because of their recent success, and you throw money away too easily without fully understanding the dynamics behind it."

He doesn't warn against angel investments entirely but advises novice angels to do their homework first. "Start to leverage the skills you have as an advisor. Find a couple of startups and entrepreneurs, and work for a bit alongside them. Then, start to do angel investments, maybe into the same companies, because then you'll be able to understand what skills you have to assess these things, and how you can bring value to make things more likely to succeed. At that point, it's much easier to assess what things you should be in, and what things you should not be into."

Why all the background research? "The risks are so high. So by being able to pick things around the criteria of what you can actually understand, you're going to increase your chances a lot of actually being successful." According to Wadstrom, getting to know "the market landscape and the other technologies involved" is the essential first step before making an angel investment.

YOUR ANGEL-INVESTING POLICY

How much should you invest?

Many of those I interviewed made small investments in a number of different companies. The successful ones carved out a discrete pot of angel investment funds in a "Risk" portfolio and never handed over money in their "Maintain" portfolio that they need to sustain their lifestyle.

Rob Nail addresses the "How much?" question by dividing his portfolio into sections. As Nail explained it, his strategy is to separate his "Risk" assets for things like angel investments, and then "not do any more than that," because this serial entrepreneur warns, "you're going to make some mistakes."

Attorney Mark Cameron White has worked closely with startups and founders for decades. He calls Nail's strategy "a success," explaining, "He's smart because he's planning." The challenge, White says, "is coming up with a portfolio of your net worth between what you risk and what's not [at risk]." Why? Because "everything in the Valley is high risk," and people who've had success crave more.

In his role as Director of Venture Capital Services at Fenwick & West, a technology and life sciences law firm, Darrell Kong saw angel investors get calls to add more money.[21] He explains that if a liquidity event does not happen, there are no exits for the investors, and the startup must "keep these things alive on life support." Kong continued, "If I'm a former name-your-company employee, and I have a couple million dollars, and I start making angel investments of $50,000 to $100,000, it seems interesting. But when these [angel-financed] companies start coming back to the well needing $3 or $4 million, and I haven't seen any exits in the meantime, am I willing to keep doing that?"

A great way to be disciplined with your investing is to have a written plan. For example, Wadstrom limits himself to an annual budget of three startups at $10,000 to $100,000 each. Have a detailed strategy before you start angel investing to avoid putting your total net worth at too much risk.

LUCK AND ANGEL INVESTING

Regardless of your past successes or failures, your confidence, or your business plan, luck can ultimately make or break an investment. So while some serial investors continue to succeed, it is important to recognize that there is no sure-fire formula. According to attorney White, "I don't care how experienced you are, you cannot tell how a company is going to do when it is first formed. You cannot tell. I've had companies that I just thought would not do anything, and they've done spectacularly well. Companies that ought to, on paper, do extremely well, have done nothing."

Entrepreneur Peter Herz thoughtfully seconds White. "I know a lot of people that have had giant successes and a lot of people who have failed miserably. There's a subset of people who think success is theirs because they're smart and hardworking, and they don't attribute, either at all or sufficiently, the role of luck in their outcomes." While it may seem tempting to assume you have the golden touch when investing in startups, giving yourself some time to conduct thorough research and committing to participate in the venture before you write a check will increase your chance of becoming a future success story.

Additionally, as a result of the successes of many entrepreneurs over the past two decades, "you've got a broader base of technology entrepreneurs and investors that have made money in prior investments. They want to reinvest, and [angel investing] is a way for them to get back into their next company. You have some entrepreneurs that made a lot of money and they just want to be investors and mentors to companies."

If you're interested in learning more about angel investing, read my book *Startup Wealth*, in which I discuss tips and traps, as revealed by experienced and successful angel investors.

FINANCIAL PLANNING AND TAX TIPS

TIP 16   Donating Appreciated Stock to Charity

The tax code currently provides an incentive for individuals to donate appreciated securities, instead of cash, to fund charitable bequests. At my firm, we advise our clients with low basis securities (holdings acquired for much less than they're worth today) to consider using them to fund the majority of their charitable donations.

In most cases, you can reduce your taxable income by the amount of gifts made to charity. For example, a donor in the 40% federal and state combined tax bracket would generally receive $400 in tax savings from a $1,000 charitable contribution. A donation of stock that is worth more than when it was purchased (or received) and held for more than a year yields a greater tax benefit than a cash donation. Such gifts of appreciated stock are deductible at the full fair market value, effectively allowing the donor to avoid paying taxes on the capital gain (appreciation).

This table illustrates the benefits of donating appreciated stock to charity. In the example, an individual donates stock or mutual funds valued at $40,000, with a cost basis of $10,000 to a charity. The cash column illustrates the tax treatment of selling the shares and donating the cash from the sale to the charity.

Comparing Charitable Gifts: Stock Versus Cash

Tax Savings	Gift of Appreciated Stock or Funds	Gift of Cash from Sale of Shares
Contribution Amount (Tax Deduction)	$40,000	$40,000
Tax Benefit of Contribution ($40,000 * 40%)	(16,000)	(16,000)
Tax on long-term capital gain from sale of investment ($30,000 * 20%) (a)	0	6,000
Net cost of gift	**$24,000**	**$30,000**

(a) Assumes a 20% combined federal and state long-term capital gain tax rate.

Figure 8. The net cost of stock and cash gifts to charity.

Gifts of appreciated securities can be made directly to a qualified charity or to a donor-advised charitable fund. A **donor-advised charitable fund** offers some unique benefits, including:

- **Reduced paperwork**—You can eliminate most of the paperwork of security transfers to multiple charities. A donation of a block of securities to the donor-advised fund is made, and you can parcel out individual donations later.

- **Take a Tax Deduction Before Granting Gifts to Charities**—Donors recognize a tax deduction for transfers made to the fund in the current tax year, while transfers to individual charities can be made in the current year or in future years. This strategy works well if you expect to be in a lower tax bracket in future years, and you want to keep the amount of your charitable contributions steady.

Donor-advised funds operate much like a private foundation without the tax return filing requirements. While individuals can contribute cash, contributing either stock or funds held for more than one year gives the biggest tax benefit. Contributions of appreciated stock or funds to the donor-advised fund receive a fair market value deduction in the year of transfer. Once an investment is received by the "sponsoring organization," such as Schwab or a community foundation, the security transferred is liquidated and placed into one or more pooled accounts selected by the donor. The donor can then use these funds to make cash gifts to charitable organizations. The gifts can be made all in one year or over several years.

Tax note: Under current tax law, a gift of appreciated stock to a charity can be deducted in the amount of 30% of your adjusted gross income (AGI); cash gifts to charities can be deducted for up to 50% of your AGI. If you make a gift in excess of these amounts, you may carry forward the deduction for five years.

TIP 17 Charitable Donation Pointers

Charitable contributions are an itemized deduction and must be shown on Schedule A of your Form 1040. You can deduct cash contributions of up to 50% of your adjusted gross income (AGI) and non-cash contributions, such as clothing or stock, up to 30% of your AGI. Itemized deductions may be limited if you are a "high-income" taxpayer.

Do you like to volunteer? Unfortunately, you are not able to deduct the value of your volunteer time on your tax return. You are, however, allowed to deduct mileage driven for charitable purposes, at 14 cents a mile (for the 2014 tax year). Let's say you visit with cancer patients on a weekly basis in a hospital 15 miles from your home. The miles that you drive from your home to the hospital for your volunteer work are a tax-deductible charitable contribution.

Keep in mind: When giving gifts and time to charity, don't let the tax tail wag the dog. Give to a charity because you like what it does. A charitable gift is still cash out of your pocket. Although the tax deduction is a nice incentive, your tax savings won't equal the full amount of the gift, and the deduction may be limited due to the phasing out of itemized deductions for high-income taxpayers.

Checklist for Startup Employees in Phase 4

FOR EVERYONE WORKING IN THE STARTUP:

- ❑ If applicable, continue to diversify your concentrated stock position into a globally diversified portfolio.

- ❑ Continue to monitor your Maintain, Risk, and Give Buckets.

- ❑ If you're interested in charity, consider from a tax perspective whether you'd like to give appreciated stock or a cash gift. Explore donor-advised funds. Consider making a charitable gift through your trust or will.

- ❑ If you're interested in angel investing, get to know the market landscape and start slowly, with small investments earmarked toward businesses you understand or have the time to explore. Avoid feeling overconfident and never dip into your Maintain portfolio for angel investing.

- ❑ Revisit your estate plan if it has been more than five years since you created it.

- ❑ Hold regular family meetings to discuss goals and wealth preservation.

- ❑ Consider what makes you happy outside of work. If you can afford it, follow your passions.

PARTNERING WITH AN ADVISOR AT ANY PHASE

WHAT'S YOUR HIGHEST AND BEST USE? Former Oracle CFO Roy Bukstein encourages people to explore the best use of their time. Are you comfortable with your level of knowledge and the time you can commit to managing your personal finances? While you're probably "capable of managing it now," he says, your situation may change over time. People get busy, go through life changes (such as having children or taking on a demanding new job), and the unexpected can happen, too. Is your spouse up to the challenge of managing your finances if you are unable to do so?

"Come to grips with the fact that you can't do it all," stresses Bukstein. If you want a high probability of achieving your goals, hiring an advisor is a smart decision. An objective advisor will keep you grounded in a volatile market and cautious in the face of a stock market that races upward very quickly.

Paying a management fee frees you up to focus on things you enjoy, so you no longer have the burden of monitoring your investments. If you have a personal financial advisor, you should receive ongoing guidance on reducing taxes and personalized advice from a professional who understands your specific situation. The benefit of a financial advisor increases as time goes on. Having someone on call who knows your situation and can answer your questions thoughtfully, with guidance customized to your circumstances, is very valuable.

John Bowen, CEO of CEG Worldwide, believes the fee paid to a financial advisor should translate into "10 times its value received by the client."[1] After spending 26 years as a Silicon Valley financial advisor and helping to manage more than $1.6 billion in assets, Bowen now runs a firm that coaches financial advisors from around the country. "The anecdotal experience is that [adding at least 10 times the value of the fees] is not a very high benchmark for top financial advisors to meet when they're delivering a world-class wealth management experience. The combination of improved return on a risk-adjusted basis, lower costs, mitigation of taxes, more effective estate planning, asset protection, and more impactful charitable planning for most clients should be well over 10 times the annual advisory fee."[2]

Benefits of Having a Personal Financial Beacon

Here's a brief—but important—list of the reasons why you should consider outsourcing your personal financial management:

- **It's a time-saver.** Any hour you are not reviewing, researching, implementing, and monitoring your investments and financial plan is time you can devote to work, family, or fun.
- **Access to the most up-to-date news and industry trends.** Your financial planner should be watching out for you and incorporating relevant news into the guidance you receive.
- **Practical knowledge blended with insight tailored to your personal situation.** With an ongoing and intimate relationship, your advisor can give you personalized answers in just a few minutes.
- **It's a one-stop solution.** Most advisors can call on a team of experts to help with the myriad of financial decisions that come up. Ideally, a financial planner should facilitate access to a strong network if outside help is needed.

Financial Planners Versus "Hair and Tooth Guys"

Independent financial planners have a different skill set than representatives of brokerage firms, sometimes known as "financial guys," who buy and sell stocks and bonds but do not have a duty to act in their clients' best interest. The SEC defines the suitability standard for an advisor as "a reasonable basis for believing that the recommendation is suitable for you." But a suitable recommendation is not necessarily the best. Contrast this with the fiduciary standard of care demanded of registered investment advisors (RIAs): "The advisor must place the client's best interest above his own."[3]

A helpful planner is able to dive deeply enough to understand your goals and values, and then establish and strengthen the client-advisor relationship with good communication and empathy—skills that are not taught in business school. Of course, a planner's ability to accurately crunch numbers to arrive at conclusions for the amount of, say, life insurance you need, or the benefit of doing a Roth IRA conversion, is a given.

In contrast, the average private client guy at a prominent investment bank is often known as a "hair and tooth guy," according to one advisor. These public-facing folks serving individual clients at many large brokerage firms are typically "not super quantitative. A lot of times, frankly, they're just sales guys."[4]

At the end of the day, the "hair and tooth guys" have to be loyal to their employers; RIAs are more likely to have your best interest at heart.

One wealthy CEO I spoke with has money invested in the private banks of five Wall Street firms.[5] With some surprise he says, "What I learned the hard way is that all these guys might have great names, and you've heard of them before, and maybe over the years they've done well, but I'm very disappointed with the returns that I've had." In the 1990s and early 2000s, when most asset classes were up, he remembered, his bankers "were in the right place at the right time." But in 2007, "the first time there was a hiccup, these guys all folded like a cheap suit."

At the private banks, said the successful CEO, there's a risk. "They just push whatever is coming down the pike, because they get such a nice commission off of it." Yet he believes, "These guys in their minds are actually trying very hard to make you money and think they're doing a good job. They have very good backgrounds and MBAs from very prestigious schools in general. So it's not like these guys are bad guys." However, he cautions that investors should understand the target market of their advisor. If you don't meet the private bank minimum, you'll get an advisor who is "down the food chain," meaning not much experience, polish, or skill.

Independently wealthy himself, the CEO acknowledged that hiring an independent advisor who is paid a percentage of assets to help clients do the right thing is a good idea, especially for someone without trading acumen.

At the Silicon Valley office of Fenwick & West, Darrell Kong knew many entrepreneurs, venture capital investors, and industry executives who had liquidity events. When I asked him how people find a financial planner, he said, "My guess is that there are a lot of financial advisors that are prospecting up and down the Peninsula. They're probably tracking the same news services that I'd use as far as seeing who has become successful, at least as far as raising the bigger rounds. You can project the companies that are doing well and just get in front of them."

If you're contacted by a salesperson to manage your financial life, be sure to ask a lot of questions. You want to make sure you're trusting your money and your life to someone whose skills and interests are firmly aligned with your goals. Keep reading for a list of probing questions to ask.

Before You Hire a Financial Planner

Increase your chances of success by taking the time to do your research before choosing a financial planner, and be sure to interview at least two candidates before you commit. Understand the fee structure, since any fees are a headwind to your portfolio returns. Below are some great questions to start you off.

- What are your financial planning credentials and designations?
- How long have you been offering financial planning services?
- What is your process for working with clients?
- Will you—or one of your associates—work directly with me on an ongoing basis?
- Do you or your firm receive financial incentives by recommending certain financial products?
- Do you offer ongoing advice regarding my non-investment financial affairs, and look at my entire financial picture?
- Do you and your firm have a fiduciary duty to act in your clients' best interest?
- Can I access my information, account balances, and performance reports on-demand?
- How are you and your firm paid? List all sources including asset management fees, trading and insurance commissions, mutual fund expense ratios, sales fees on mutual funds with loads, and revenue sharing with business partners.

Hiring a financial planner is a commitment that should be taken seriously; you should only do it after a significant amount of research. You might also want to consider the following before you hire:

- Read the firm's website. Does the tone of the communication resonate with you? Do the steps outlined and process described make sense?

- Does the firm do real, analysis-intensive financial planning looking at your assets and annual cash flow projections?

- Will the advisors project what your cash flow and assets look like in the future? Will they project children's educational expenses? Do they show these projections in today's dollars (not future dollars)? And will they provide you with backup for their conclusions?

- Do the advisors prepare an after-tax cash flow projection to determine how much you can add to your portfolio? Or do they take shortcuts and ask you to estimate—or worse, just guess—how much excess cash you have?

- Do they anticipate—and ask about—lifestyle changes as part of your long-term plan, such as additional vacation in retirement or childcare costs if you are about to start a family?

- Do the advisors have a team of experts, such as attorneys and CPAs, available to assist you?

- Are the financial planning and investment management fees reasonable? Many independent advisors believe total fees above 1% (on the value of a portfolio of at least $500,000) are too high, and that for portfolios above $2 million, the break-point fee for managing assets above that amount should be less than 1%. This fee should include financial planning, or else it should be lower.

- Do the advisors recommend funds from the universe of mutual funds, or do they favor proprietary funds packaged and sold by their firm? Proprietary funds generally have high fees and are sold to captive clients.

- Does the firm serve people in a similar situation to yours?

- How does the firm report on your performance—by total portfolio, by account, or by holding? The most transparent reporting method is to compare the returns of the total portfolio (all accounts, combined) after fees to a blended benchmark representing your risk profile.

- During your interviews with potential advisors, are their questions designed to learn about your holdings so that they can sell a financial product? Or are they designed to help them understand you, your family, and your comfort with risk?

Additional Advisor Advantages

A knowledgeable and experienced financial planner can add plenty of value. A competent advisor can:

- **Look out for you.** While it's important to look out for yourself, it can be extremely helpful to have a professional double-check your decisions and calculations to make sure you are protected.
- **Reduce your taxes.** Loss harvesting (see page 125) and thoughtful placement of holdings can create a tax-efficient investment portfolio.
- **Serve as your personal CFO.** Your personal financial manager can lead or direct your personal financial affairs and coordinate interaction between various advisors, such as accountants, attorneys, and insurance brokers.
- **Mitigate worry.** A professional advisor can oversee the daily activity of your investments and make changes as soon as they are needed.
- **Help with cash flow planning.** In cash-flush times, an advisor can help you look at cash flow to determine your surplus for the year and, when possible, add the excess to your long-term savings. In lean-cash years, an advisor can formulate a tax-efficient strategy for raising cash or cutting expenses to meet ongoing needs.
- **Keep you invested during jittery markets, and help you reap the rewards of long-term equity returns.** (See "Annualized Investor Returns Versus Benchmarks" on page 116.)
- **Track progress toward your goals.**
- **Protect what you've earned.** Having adequate protection and insurance—for yourself and your property—ensures your assets will not be taken away in a lawsuit.
- **Simplify your life by consolidating multiple accounts.**

- **Help create strategies for passing assets to heirs.**
- **Create a plan to save for your children's college education in a tax-advantageous way.**

What Clients Say
About Working with a Professional Financial Planner

Whether delegation comes easily to you or you are willing to try it for the expectation of a better life, read on to discover the benefits of professional management directly from a handful of interviewees for this book. Names have been changed, and comments have been condensed for clarity.

ANDREW

Andrew, a 40-something Senior Engineering Director at a Bay Area Internet company, has been with his financial planner since before the company's IPO. He lists many reasons for working with a professional financial planner. First and foremost, he said, "I was looking for guidance and wanted an advisor who was a good communicator."

Here are some additional reasons Andrew likes to work with a financial planner:

- I appreciate the cyclical nature of annual planning meetings.
- Action items are addressed in each meeting, and there is follow-up annually—at least.
- It's time-consuming to develop expertise in financial and tax planning, and all of my time is either spent at work or with my wife and our dog. My advisor makes financial education understandable.
- My advisor is patient with me; if I do not act on all of the advisor's suggestions, either because of lack of time or not understanding, she'll remind me of the importance.
- My advisor is persistent about reminding me about outstanding action items.
- A deep understanding about stock options and other equity awards translates into a mindful approach to the tax issues surrounding action with equity awards. My advisor's familiarity with my company's equity awards means immediate comprehension of new equity grants.

FRAN

C-suite executive Fran, who works 60-hour weeks, said her advisor is "competent and expert in her field, and I love that she's highly organized. She follows up. She's professional in the preparation of reports and presentations. Her staff is prompt to provide attention when asked. They don't take a cookie-cutter approach."

The prime advantages Fran and her husband have enjoyed by working with the advisor include:

- Confidence about having the assets they need when they're ready to retire. The advisor got them on a solid track 10 years before retirement. The advisor has a dynamic process of checking in and updating goals, since goals change.
- The advisor provides motivation to help them achieve their long-term goals.
- The management fee paid "is an investment, not a cost. My advisor's unique value is that planning is not a static process, and they are always validating and revalidating goals."

GEORGE

George, a human resources executive, said, "The most important thing in my family's relationship with a financial advisor is trust. While they monitor my portfolio and report on returns, most of my evaluation of my advisor is done by watching body language, asking questions, and assessing how deep and how strong her responses are." One of his concerns about managing his finances on his own is doing "something stupid." He acknowledges, "I'm not a financial genius, and if managing my own portfolio, I'd be susceptible to all kinds of awful things," like scams and less-than-ideal investments. The major benefit he and his wife appreciate in their work with an advisor is "relaxing about our future."

INGRID

Ingrid is an MBA, attorney, and high-tech executive. She and her husband are great savers, using a portion of the proceeds from the IPO of the company Ingrid worked for to purchase a modest house in a neighborhood with a great school system for their two young children. Before they found their current advisor, they were clients of a big national brokerage firm, chosen because the firm was the underwriter for her company's IPO. Over time, Ingrid became very disappointed with the investments the firm singled out for her family. Most disappointing, her advisor was not willing to stick by her side and talk through her fears during the 2008/2009 market downtown. Ingrid sold a large portion of her holdings at the bottom of the bear market and lost out on the bounce back.

Ingrid's thoughts on hiring an advisor include:

- Paying an investment advisory fee is "the premium for the time that I now gain."

- The fear for those who've never used an advisor, or for those who've had a disappointing investment experience is, "Does the fee that I'm paying justify the increase in returns that you would have gotten, or I would have gotten, if I was doing it myself?

- "I want to make sure it's taken care of. I don't have time to do this myself anymore, and I want somebody who would do it as well or better than I would, who will be responsive and trustworthy, and understand what I've been through to accumulate this money and what's necessary to allow me to hold on to it."

- Performance is a tricky subject. You don't want an advisor to take on too much risk with your portfolio, yet risk is how large returns happen. Getting the balance of the risk level of her and her husband right requires knowledge and empathy. "There's a lot of sensitivity, there's a lot of judgment," says this client about her experience with her current advisor.

You will experience ups and downs in your portfolio, but a long-term financial plan will give you confidence about your future.

Be Sure You're Getting Financial Planning Advice: Regulation of the Financial Services Industry

We rely on the government to protect our food and water supply. Unfortunately, at this time we can't rely on the government to completely oversee the financial industry.

"Financial advisor" and "financial planner" are titles used loosely. The U.S.

government does not regulate the use of either. Instead, financial services professionals are regulated by the services they provide. For example, a planner who also provides securities advice is regulated as a stockbroker or investment advisor. As a result, the term "financial planner" may be used in a way that is confusing to consumers.

However, credentials from regulatory agencies and professional associations can be relied upon to explain experience and knowledge. Professional designations are awarded to individuals after intensive training and testing, eliminating potential consumer confusion. Here are definitions of some popular designations:

- **CFP®—CERTIFIED FINANCIAL PLANNER™.** Individuals must have a college degree, work 6,000 hours under strict experience guidelines or 4,000 hours as an apprentice,[6] pass certification classes, and pass a rigorous two-day board exam.

- **CFA—Chartered Financial Analyst.** This credential is focused primarily on investments. CFA Charterholders, as they are called, must have four years of investment work experience and complete three six-hour exams. The CFA is a credential that indicates a depth of investment expertise as well as a vigorous code of ethics and fiduciary duty.

- **CPA—Certified Public Accountant.** Individuals must pass a rigorous exam focused on taxes, accounting, auditing, and business law. Additionally, education and work experience requirements vary by state.

- **CLU—The Chartered Life Underwriter** designation is held by life insurance salespeople.

- **ChFC—A Chartered Financial Consultant** credential requires classes but no comprehensive board exam.[7]

Education, credentials, and experience do matter. Often people in the investment advisory business were trained in another discipline before entering the field. Choose someone who has a technical background such as accounting, engineering, or finance, and say no to working with a former car salesperson or real estate broker.

FEE-ONLY ADVISORS

Fee-only advisors are compensated by clients only, and not from mutual fund or insurance commissions, referral fees, or kickbacks from vendors. Receiving compensation based solely on assets under management or on an hourly basis means the advisor has your best interests in mind and is free of bias toward or against any particular investment or insurance product. The opposite of fee-only is "fee-based," meaning that commissions are accepted.

Resources for Finding the Best Advisor for You

What's the best way to choose an advisor?

In addition to asking for recommendations from trusted friends, colleagues, and family, search for planners where they are: on the websites of their professional associations. Be sure to understand each advisor's specialty or niche area.

A CERTIFIED FINANCIAL PLANNER™ professional is the gold standard in the professional financial advisor world. Earning the CFP® certification means the advisor has joined a select group of competent and ethical personal financial planning advisors.

THE CERTIFIED FINANCIAL PLANNER BOARD OF STANDARDS (CFP.net)

A CFP® practitioner is required to act in your best interest. Only those who have fulfilled the certification and renewal requirements of the CFP Board can display the CFP® certification trademarks, which represent a high level of competency, ethics, and professionalism. Read more about the CFP® certification and the importance of the designation on this website.

THE FINANCIAL PLANNING ASSOCIATION (FPAnet.org)

Find a financial planner using the resources on this site. The Financial Planning Association® (FPA®) is a membership organization for CFP® professionals in the United States. Members adhere to the highest standards of professional competence, ethical conduct, and clear, complete disclosure to those they serve.

THE NATIONAL ASSOCIATION OF PERSONAL FINANCIAL ADVISORS (NAPFA.org)

This is a membership organization of fee-only financial advisors. Each member must take a fiduciary oath to act in the good faith and in the best interests of the client, and does not receive any compensation that is contingent on any client's purchase or sale of a financial product.[8]

THE GARRETT PLANNING NETWORK (GarrettPlanningNetwork.com)

The Garrett Planning Network has an hourly-based model. Check out the financial planners in the network for a once-a-year review or ongoing assistance.

FINANCIAL PLANNING AND TAX TIPS

TIP 18   The Best Way to Find an Honest Advisor

Below, I provide a few ways to help ensure that you are dealing with an advisor who is aboveboard. Honest advisors will gladly comply with these standards and answer your questions. Those with something to hide may deviate from these practices or claim their investment process is "proprietary" or "too technical" to concern yourself with, as financial con man Bernie Madoff claimed to inquisitive prospective clients.

- Make sure you have access to your account through the custodian's website. Custodians are firms like Charles Schwab (and the advisory arm, Schwab Institutional), Fidelity, and TDAmeritrade. It's great if you can see your account balance and performance reports through your advisor's site, too, but make sure you can review your holdings online via a third-party custodian. This way, you can be sure you own what the advisor's statement says.

- The custodian of your assets should have financial statements audited by a U.S.-based auditor. The custodian's financial statements should not be just "reviewed" or "compiled," as these are lower standards than a full audit.

- Ask questions about where and why assets are custodied at certain firms. Assets should never be held at the advisor's firm (unless the firm also operates as a custodian), and never with the same party who directs the accounts.

- Confirm that monthly or quarterly statements will be delivered online or by mail from a third-party custodian, not the money manager.

- Understand how your assets are safeguarded, and who the advisor shares information with other than you. Information is often shared through paper or electronic reports, or via web access through the advisor's client portal in addition to the custodian's website.

- The potential advisor (or someone at the firm) should patiently respond to any and all questions about investment philosophy, asset allocation, and risk. Educational questions are an important way to gauge comfort with an advisor. (See "Before You Hire a Financial Planner" beginning on page 160 for a list of questions.)
- The advisor should be able to provide backup for the work performed on your behalf, such as detailed year-by-year cash flow projections when preparing a retirement or life insurance analysis, and the formula used to calculate your investment performance.
- Ideally, the advisor will clearly state fees on performance reports. Performance should be shown net of fees, unless otherwise stated.
- Your accounts should be in your own name and not commingled with the assets of other clients or in the name of the firm.
- Ask for references from existing long-term clients in a similar life or career situation to you (for example, high-tech executives with stock-option planning issues, or divorced women). Contact at least two longtime clients to ask about ongoing access and services.
- You should feel comfortable talking with the advisor. Your advisor should understand your goals and values, and talking to that person should be a pleasant and not at all concerning experience.
- If the advisor uses mutual funds, exchange traded funds (ETFs), and/or publicly traded stocks and trades through a known outside custodian, this would indicate a low risk of shifty behavior—that is, a high chance your assets are safe from pilfering or Ponzi schemes. However, the skills of stock picking and/or asset allocation still must be assessed.

At the end of the day, hiring an advisor is a leap of faith. However, doing your due diligence and using the information presented in this section should give you a very high degree of confidence about moving forward.

CONCLUSION

THROUGHOUT THIS BOOK, YOU'VE LEARNED about how lucky high-tech employees who arrive at a liquidity event are often unprepared to deal with the sudden financial and emotional consequences. That's why if you anticipate finding yourself in that position, it's crucial to create a plan early on that will help preserve your wealth so that you can reach your goals.

Phase 1 is maniacally busy and stressful as you funnel all your resources into the company. It's also an important time to project your personal cash flow, consider early exercising your stock options and restricted stock, and evaluate your commitment to the startup. In Phase 2, when you and your team are ramping up to an IPO, merger, or acquisition, you'll want to be prepared for last-minute surprises before the deal is finalized. Spending before you have cash in your bank account is like playing with fire—you've waited this long, so don't ruin your financial future at the last minute. As explained in the disastrous tale of the Bakers losing their popular Dragon Systems software and the equity they built up over decades of hard work, enlisting trustworthy financial and legal assistance and doing due diligence on each party involved in the deal can help prevent a clash of motives and can make sure you don't lose out.

After a liquidity event, things change. Depending on your exit type and contractual obligations, you may see shifts in management or in your own position with the company. You may make big purchases. These significant career, financial, and emotional transitions make an even greater case for you to carefully consider your next move. Whether you stay on at the company during Phase 3, it's crucial to concentrate on protecting your wealth in Phases 3 and 4. Avoid attachment issues of holding on to company stock based on fear or greed, because that's an all-too-common way to lose what you've worked so hard for. In fact, selling at least half of your equity as soon as you can is a strategy used successfully by many who have preserved their wealth. Using a decision tree analysis can help open your eyes to what's at stake if you're contemplating selling your stock.

Diversification away from a concentrated position in company stock is not a comment about your faith; it's a smart financial decision that ensures you have a financial cushion if the value of your stock unexpectedly implodes. Before spending the tangible value of your efforts in the startup via cash in your hand, understand your goals and resources. Divide your assets into Maintain, Risk, and Give Buckets, and execute your plan with appropriate levels of risk and global diversification.

In every phase of a startup, my interviewees stressed the importance of being extremely disciplined about money management—or hiring an advisor to be disciplined for you. Even most who said they could be unemotional about their own company stock told me they outsource to advisors, anyway. One reason is that what you don't know *can* hurt you. Even if you have the time to watch the market and do research every day, most people just don't have the education and experience professional financial planners have. So if an opportunity comes along to save tens or hundreds of thousands of dollars through smart tax and financial planning, you may miss it managing your own finances.

For the majority of people, however, the more important reason for handing their personal finances over to a competent professional is that they'd rather have more time to focus on what they love: their favorite hobbies, their company or work, and their family. If you only have two free hours a day—or week!—to begin with, wouldn't you rather spend that time on what makes you happy?

Unfortunately, many high-tech employees dedicate themselves so fully to their work that they don't even know what makes them happy and have trouble finding motivation and purpose in life after a liquidity event. The best way to avoid feeling listless and unfulfilled during this period is to have a post-liquidity plan in which you identify—in advance—your passions and how you are going to pursue them. This plan can be very difficult to create in the midst of 16-hour workdays ramping up to an IPO or buyout.

The Four Phases of Startup Life[SM]

Phase 1	Phase 2	Liquidity Event	Phase 3	Phase 4
Pre-Transition 2-40 years Laying the Foundation	**Pre-Transition** 0-24 months Ramping Up		**Post-Transition** 1-24 months Realizing the Dream	**Into the Future** 2-40 years What's Next?

Quality of Life Challenges

Phase 1	Phase 2		Phase 3	Phase 4
Preoccupation with startup Loneliness Optimism Tenacity	Maintaining balance while working long hours Excitement Persistence		Weighing career options If you stay: Vest in peace and maintain work-life balance If you leave: Figure out what's next	Flexibility and choices Charitable activities Travel New career or startup Passion projects

Financial Challenges

Phase 1	Phase 2		Phase 3	Phase 4
Raising capital Below-market salary Accountability to investors Funnel all resources to create and build the company	Increasing enterprise value Salary and bonus Accountability to investors, management, and board Planning with equity awards		Increasing enterprise value and stock price Accountability to shareholders, board, and management Diversification of concentrated position Expensive purchases	New or second home Venture or angel investing Strategizing goals with financial resources

Common to All Phases

Challenge	Maximize Value of Equity Awards (ISO, NQ, RSA, RSU, ESPP)
Concerns	Wealth Preservation Tax Reduction Wealth Protection Passing Assets to Heirs Charitable Giving
Solutions	Personal CFO Expert Team of Advisors Financial Education

I've created a guide to help you start as soon as you can, and refine as time goes on. I call the process of discovering and planning for life before and after an IPO or other wealth event **BE WISE: Before Event, Work, Identify, Strategize, Execute**. This formula helps you understand what's important to you early on, guiding you in the best direction—for you. Later, through thoughtfully addressing each area of the BE WISE Planning Strategy, you can spend your time post-liquidity event feeling happy and fulfilled, with assurance that your assets will cover your long-term needs. The BE WISE Planning Strategy white paper is available at JLFwealth.com, where you can find more detail on this topic and other tips for wise planning.

Finally, if you are an entrepreneur, be sure to read my book *Startup Wealth* for founder-focused guidance about making smart financial decisions.

THE BE WISE PLANNING STRATEGY™

WHAT MOTIVATES YOU TO GET UP each morning, excited to greet the day and make a difference?

To have a satisfying life, it's important to identify your passions. This process, in combination with the effective use of your financial resources, is crucial for personal happiness. This appendix is adapted from a white paper that discusses the BE WISE Planning Strategy for financial and personal success.

The process of discovering and planning for life before and after a wealth event is detailed in the acronym **BE WISE: Before Event, Work, Identify, Strategize, Execute**. While the last two stages are chronological—your plan is analyzed, then action steps are created and executed—Work and Identify should happen together. See the graphic on page 177.

Here is a closer look at how the BE WISE Planning Strategy can help you think through your choices.

BE WISE

BEFORE EVENT

Creating and building a company starts with a business plan. Here, however, it's important to identify what you want out of your career and what kind of company you want to build. Mergers and acquisitions attorney Marlee Myers agrees. "When you're starting a business, it's very important to think through what kind of business you want this to be. Do you want to have a small business that's run by a very close team achieving certain economic objectives, scientific objectives, or even social objectives?" Or are you "looking to have a large public company or a great big payday," in which case "you would do things differently, and you would think about your capital structure differently, and you would think about your business model differently. No matter what, you need to think about how many employees you want to have, and what sort of policies you want to implement, and whether or not you want to share equity."

My research shows that knowing what you want out of your career—and making sure that it's something you're passionate about—is fundamental to success. Thinking through your life goals well before a liquidity event will help you survive the stress you can anticipate as you ramp up toward an event and enjoy the freedom of a big exit.

BE WISE
WORK

The next step is to create and build your company. The timeline varies for this step—between two and 40 years, according to many interviewees, and although there is no single formula for success, a great team is crucial. This phase can be very emotional. In addition to constant preoccupation with the startup and sometimes loneliness, this time can be satisfying for those who love startup life (see the Four Phases of a Startup Life chart on page 173 for more details).

BE WISE
IDENTIFY YOUR ESSENCE

Before or during the building of your company, determine what is important to you and what your personal goals are. If you are fortunate enough to one day have a liquidity event, how would you fill your time? Without such a post-liquidity plan, many executives who've had a quick exit after an IPO or buyout become despondent and may have trouble hanging on to their savings.

Planning is the key. "If you can identify your passion, you can identify what you want to do and be, and that helps you be successful," says Honorary Czech Consul General Richard Pivnicka. "For example, my passion in life wasn't being a lawyer. That was a job—admittedly a very good job," he recalls, explaining that

The **BE WISE** Planning Strategy™

Before Event
Create a business plan incorporating your goals for your company and your career, which will likely include some of your personal values.

Work
Build your company. Consult with a CPA or comprehensive financial planner about tax planning with your equity awards. Entrepreneurs: Strategize the ideal corporate and equity award structure, and hire an attorney to create contracts, early exercise elections, and vesting schedules.

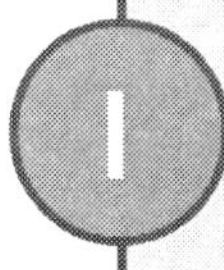

Identify
Identify what's important to you. How will you spend your time if your company is sold, acquired, or goes public? Don't be caught without a plan.

Strategize
Determine if your assets will support your goals and values. Carve out a "Maintain Bucket" for long-term lifestyle needs. Allocate excess capital into "Risk," "Give," and other buckets, if needed.

Execute
Implement and monitor specific action items as a road map to achieve your goals, preserve your wealth, minimize risk and taxes, and pass along assets to those you care about.

he decided to become a lawyer because of the expectations for high-achieving students like him. "I ended up gravitating from law to real estate because it was more fun. You have a beautiful building when you're done, you help people find a place to live, it's creative, and it's not just about money, which law is all about." Pivnicka and his wife have won awards for their restorations of historic homes, including the Mark Hopkins family mansion in Atherton, California.[1]

Likely, what will make you happy is the same thing that always has, so think back to your past interests and evaluate what you liked doing most. Articulate your personal life plan as soon as possible. In business, you have a business plan, a budget, and a timeline. Why shouldn't the same type of forethought and strategy go into your personal life?

BE WISE

STRATEGIZE: MAINTAIN, RISK & GIVE

If you know where you want to go, a financial plan can help you highlight any gaps that may exist along the way. Strategizing your goals and how to use your assets should occur directly after a liquidity event. The timing is important, because if too much time goes by post-liquidity, you may lose out on planning and wealth-creation opportunities. Here you will determine, through quantitative analysis, if your assets will support your goals, values, and interests for the remainder of your life. If you have excess, you get to decide what to do with this pot of funds—the cherry on top.

To protect your finances and reach these goals, divide your wealth into two or three categories, or buckets.

❶ **The Maintain Bucket.** The first bucket should consist of what you need to comfortably live out your life. This money is what you need to maintain your lifestyle, and extensive analytical work, often under the guidance of a financial planner, should be done to determine this amount. Never dip into this pile for extra angel investment capital or other risky ventures. It's crucial to make sure the assets in your Maintain portfolio to fund your future lifestyle are invested in a prudent, risk-appropriate way.

❷ The Risk Bucket. The second pot contains exploration funds; you can use this money for angel investing, self-managed investments, starting a new company—whatever you like. *This second pot should never be merged with the first.* Make sure you have enough money to support your lifestyle, even if all of your Risk Bucket investments fail.

❸ The Give Bucket. If you are charitably inclined, the third pot is for making donations to your favorite causes.

Strategizing your personal finances is discussed in detail beginning on page 87.

BE WISE

EXECUTE

You've now determined where you are and have a vision for where you want to be. At this point, you have identified your goals, strategized how much you need to carve out for each goal, and determined how much excess you can play with. You have everything you need to move forward and execute your plan. So do it.

Invest in a portfolio that is aggressive enough to achieve your goals—some very wealthy individuals need not take on any risk, but most investors will need to take on some to stay ahead of inflation—but not so risky that you can't sleep at night. (However, some people may need to sleep less well now in order to *not* eat less well later on.)

Just Do It

When it comes to a concentrated position in stock of your company, some people cite nostalgia, taxes, and potential growth as reasons to hold. You can fulfill the nostalgia goal by retaining a token minimal number of shares—or in the extreme, you can frame one physical share certificate. Tax laws are constantly changing, and staying on top of these changes will help to maximize your post-liquidity wealth.

Read on for an example of how one high-tech entrepreneur used the BE WISE Planning Strategy to fulfill his passion.

PROFILE

INNOVATING IN UNEXPECTED AND UNUSUAL WAYS: MITCH KAPOR

FOUNDED LOTUS DEVELOPMENT CORPORATION. TOOK COMPANY PUBLIC IN 1983. SOLD TO IBM IN 1995 FOR $3.5 BILLION.

Mitch Kapor, the visionary software designer who founded Lotus Development Corporation, is a great example of someone who is using his wealth from the creation and sale of his company to achieve his philanthropic goals.[2] Kapor took his company public in 1983, based on the success of Lotus 1-2-3, the first user-friendly spreadsheet software. In 1995, IBM bought Lotus for $3.5 billion.[3]

Kapor now devotes his time to two organizations: Kapor Capital, which invests in tech startup companies dedicated to making the world a better place through positive social impact, and the nonprofit educational organization Level Playing Field Institute, which operates the Summer Math and Sciences Honors Academy (SMASH), which he co-founded with his wife, Freada Kapor Klein, to provide opportunities to high-potential low-income high school students.

Kapor's deeply held values have shaped his life path, including his philanthropy. His dedication to giving stems from his belief that "we cannot stand aside, we must engage. We may not get over the finish line, but we are here to do what we need to do while we are here." Likewise, his essence has clearly had a large hand in determining where his money goes. Through both Kapor Capital and SMASH, he helps people who "are not any different than [he is]. If you look beyond the surface—age, gender, class, race—it's all about the talent that comes in unlikely and outsider packages." Those he assists, Kapor says, "want the same things that I wanted: a chance to be accepted for who they are, and a chance to make the most of their lives to develop and to contribute."

How Does Mitch Kapor Fit into
The BE WISE Planning Strategy?

BE: Kapor incorporated the **BE** of the BE WISE Planning Strategy by building Lotus Development Corporation around his core values, including treating his employees well.

W: Creating and building the "killer app" of the 1980s allowed Mitch's **Work** to culminate in the sale of his company for $3.5 billion.

I: Kapor credits his wife, Freada, for helping him move through the **Identify** stage of the BE WISE Planning Strategy after his liquidity event. She is his "partner and inspiration and guide" for his current vision of philanthropy and business and "life partner, whom I love dearly, for a shared commitment to values, and lots of hard work with many mistakes: two steps forward, one step back." After a decade of exploration in the **I** stage, "That's how we've gotten where we've gotten," Kapor says.

S and **E:** It appears that Kapor has successfully implemented the **Strategize** and **Execute** stages, as he continues to live his dual dreams of helping young, gifted math and science students who come from less fortunate backgrounds realize their potential and helping entrepreneurs change the world through socially and economically strong ideas.

Full disclosure: Mitch Kapor is not a client of my firm.

Kapor described the chance he was given to make the most of his exceptional gifts in a speech titled "Outsiderness, Success, and Giving Back," in May 2012 at the Jewish Community Federation Business Leadership Council in San Francisco. Growing up on Long Island, New York, he felt like a "double outsider," for being both Jewish and academically advanced (notwithstanding the fact that he was physically smaller than his peers, as he had skipped second grade). In 1966, at age 15,

Kapor attended a six-week Summer Science Program in Southern California funded by the U.S. government in an effort to keep up with the Russians during the Space Race. That initial exposure to computers changed his life, and today Kapor is compelled to practice reciprocity.

SMASH does just that. This hands-on program for low-income high schoolers of color interested in math and science gives students what Kapor got out of his summer camp, and what they have never had before: a chance to be accepted by their peers, and a place where they can be challenged with high expectations.

Kapor's support of diversity continues through Kapor Capital, which supports entrepreneurs who create both economic and social value. He sums up his for-profit venture capital firm succinctly: "Entrepreneurs, it's said, scratch their own itches. Entrepreneurs who come from a different kind of background are likely to have a different set of itches, and are likely to be innovative in unexpected and unusual kinds of ways, and those are the kinds of folks we want to work with."

Kapor has always included these social values in his work. In his business plan for Lotus, he stated that the human part is as important to him as the profits. In fact, Eastern values of self-actualization were so important to him that he named his company Lotus and used a logo reminiscent of the lotus flower.

Alongside Steve Jobs and Bill Gates, Kapor has a star on the Entrepreneur's Walk of Fame in Cambridge, Massachusetts. His plaque reads, "Building a workplace which engages a diversity of employees and brings out their best makes a far greater contribution than financial success alone." He is proud of the diverse culture and values he and his team developed at Lotus.

In addition to his devotion to Eastern teachings, Kapor feels he has also absorbed Jewish ethics into his business practices through osmosis. He recently began reading Jewish texts and didn't realize all that he already knew, including, he says, the guidance to "'Let your fellow's money be as precious as your own' (from Pirkei Avot), which means to treat the person on the other side of the transaction with the same respect and dignity as you would want to be treated." Additionally, Kapor says that in our society, "We celebrate the winners, but we don't always think about the price of winning." At Lotus and in his current ventures, treating people well is part of the journey.

■ ■ ■ ■

BE WISE Conclusion

In the high-tech community, many people personally know someone who struck gold, bought a nice car, and retired—only to end up unfulfilled. Financial wealth does not constitute success; leading a happy and fulfilled life does. Mitch Kapor is just one success story. He identified his passions early and built a life full of what he loves. If you are preparing for a liquidity event, start identifying your passions. This way, after you realize financial independence, your next step forward will be to execute your personal life plan using the BE WISE Planning Strategy. Download the white paper at JLFwealth.com.

ACKNOWLEDGMENTS

This book's unique appeal derives from the generosity of those who shared their experiences working in a startup or advising those who do.

I'd like to thank those who sat for interviews and shared their wisdom and perspectives. They include Sam Adler, John Bowen, Dave Buchanan, Roy Bukstein, Lise Buyer, Ed Callan, Jonathan Cardella, Robert Carter, Mitch Cohen, Stephanie Coutu, Ed Deibert, Lara Druyan, Martin Eberhard, Leland Fong, Eliot Franklin, Mark Galant, Rachel Garb, Eric Gold, Ken Goldman, Jason Graham, Peter Herz, Michael Irvine, Darrell Kong, Jim Koshland, Danny Krebs, Jamis MacNiven, Dee Anna McPherson, Lesa Mitchell, Marlee Myers, Rob Nail, Lee Pantuso, Sonja Hoel Perkins, Richard Pivnicka, Joe Preis, Brendan Richardson, Laura Roden, Stephen Roth, Jeff Russakow, Alexandra Derby Salkin, Santosh Sharan, Tiffany Shlain, David Spark, David Stern, Marc Tarpenning, Nicolai Wadstrom, Rebecca Watson, Bill Weihl, Mark Cameron White, Bruce Wilford, Sylvia Yam, and others who spoke to me confidentially, on background.

I'd also like to thank the following:

My longtime editor, Karen Sulkis, who is a master of turning technical financial subjects into lively, pithy, accessible prose. Karen always meets deadlines and is a great friend.

Tarren Schaar, who I've had the pleasure of working with since 2008, plays a crucial role in our firm on a daily basis. Tarren has been dedicated to serving our clients and making the back office run smoothly. He also read and provided feedback on draft chapters of this book.

Intern Nicole Bauthier helped to streamline a 500-page manuscript into two focused books. She did so with bubbly enthusiasm and a strategic understanding of how books should flow. Rachel Davidson provided further editorial guidance and assistance. Samantha Hoyle was dedicated during production.

The hundreds of clients I have served over two decades, for their trust and confidence. My clients have allowed me to make a positive impact on their lives by guiding them toward their goals and dreams.

My financial planner colleagues. I'm fortunate to work in a helping profession in which sharing with other advisors benefits the community at large. The following individuals, most of whom are CERTIFIED FINANCIAL PLANNER™ professionals, read drafts of white papers and chapters and provided invaluable feedback: Sandra Bragar, Ketan Desai, Colin Drake, Robert Gavrich, David Gilbert, Emilie Goldman, Janet Hoffmann, Gretchen Hollstein, Heather Hutchinson, Bob Lee, Eric Leve, Brian Pon, and Greg Schick.

An extra-special thank-you to Tim Kochis. Tim, a luminary in the financial planning profession and an accomplished and well-respected author himself, provided feedback on the book outline and my first white paper containing preliminary research for the books.

The Kauffman Foundation, for sponsoring research to help entrepreneurs and startups succeed, and for granting me permission to use some of their findings and graphics in my books.

Samuel Roth, for sharing his decades of business wisdom, and Vanessa Bertini, for her creative inspiration.

Joe Preis and Mark Galant for book title ideas, and Peter Herz for introducing me to the decision tree concept.

Nola Miller, Kyri McClellan, Diane Ettelson, and Greg Sigel for important introductions.

My book publication team of Holly Brady, Vicky Vaughn Shea, Glenn Randle, Carrie Wicks, Mitchell Design, and Terry Franklin.

Thank you to Random House President and Publisher Gina Centrello, who read an early draft of my manuscript and offered invaluable guidance.

Additionally, the following legal, tax, and business professionals provided feedback on the technical sections of the book: John Advani, Paul Allen, Sam Berde, Frank Kearney, Beth Kramer, and Nancy Peck.

Finally, to my husband, Stephen Roth, for allowing me to share the story of his successful liquidity event and the wise planning we did, and for supporting my multiyear dedication to researching and writing two books.

SOURCES

One-Month U.S. Treasury Bills: Total returns in USD. January 1926–Present: One-Month U.S. Treasury Bills. Source: Morningstar. Former Source: Stocks, Bonds, Bills, and Inflation, Chicago: Ibbotson and Sinquefield, 1986.

Long-Term Government Bonds: Total returns net of all fees in USD. January 1926–Present: Long-Term Government Bonds. Source: Morningstar. Former Source: Stock, Bonds, Bills, and Inflation, Chicago: Ibbotson and Sinquefield, 1986.

Long-Term Corporate Bonds: Total returns net of all fees in USD. January 1926–Present: Long-Term Corporate Bonds. Source: Morningstar. Former Source: Stocks, Bonds, Bills, and Inflation, Chicago: Ibbotson and Sinquefield, 1986.

Large-Cap Stocks (S&P 500 Index): Total returns in USD. January 1990–Present: S&P 500 Index.

The S&P Data are provided by Standard & Poor's Index Services Group. January 1926–December 1989: S&P 500 Index. Ibbotson data courtesy of © Stocks, Bonds, Bills and Inflation Yearbook™, Ibbotson Associates, Chicago (annually updated works by Roger C. Ibbotson and Rex A. Sinquefield).

Small-Cap Stocks (CRSP 9-10 Index): CRSP, total returns in USD$. Small Company Universe Returns (Deciles 9 & 10)—All Exchanges. Oct. 1988–Present: CRSP Deciles 9-10 Cap-Based Portfolio. Jan. 1973–Sep. 1988: CRSP Database (NYSE & AMEX & OTC), Rebalanced Quarterly. July 1962–Dec. 1972: CRSP Database (NYSE & AMEX), Rebalanced Quarterly. Jan. 1926–June 1962: NYSE, Rebalanced Semi-Annually.

ENDNOTES

Preface

1. "Autodesk—Company," accessed November 1, 2012, http://www.autodesk.com/company.

2. David K. Randall, "March 9, 2009: The Day Stocks Bottomed Out," *Forbes*, last updated March 8, 2010, accessed January 8, 2014, http://www.forbes.com/2010/03/06/march-bear-market-low-personal-finance-march-2009.html.

3. Based on the performance of the Russell 3000 Index through December 31, 2013.

Introduction

1. Interview with entrepreneur and executive, 2012. Name withheld by mutual agreement.

Phase 1: Laying the Foundation

1. Laura Sydell, "Intel Legends Moore and Grove: Making It Last," NPR, last updated April 6, 2012, accessed January 17, 2014, http://www.npr.org/2012/04/06/150057676/intel-legends-moore-and-grove-making-it-last.

2. Ibid.

3. Peter Herz, in discussion with the author, July and August 2012.

4. Eric Gold, in discussion with the author, March 2012.

5. Roy Bukstein, in discussion with the author, December 2011.

6. Marc Tarpenning, in discussion with the author, February 2012.

7. Interview with high-tech employee, 2012. Name withheld by mutual agreement.

8. Aaron Levie, Twitter post, November 8, 2012, 10:39 p.m., http://twitter.com/levie.

9. Dave Buchanan, in discussion with the author, August 2012.

10. Interview with high-tech employee, 2012. Name withheld by mutual agreement.

11. Interview with attorney and high-tech executive, 2012. Name withheld by mutual agreement.

12. Bruce Wilford, in discussion with the author, May 2012.

13. Ed Callan, in discussion with the author, October 2011.

14. Jason Graham, in discussion with the author, July 2012.

15. Michael Irvine, in discussion with the author, August 2012.

16. Interview with attorney and high-tech executive, 2012. Name withheld by mutual agreement.

17. Irvine, interview.

18. Interview with attorney and high-tech executive, 2012. Name withheld by mutual agreement.

19. "Constructive dismissal," *Wikipedia*, accessed November 29, 2012, http://en.wikipedia.org/wiki/
     Constructive_dismissal.

20. Danny Krebs, email message to author, December 2, 2013.

21. Danny Krebs, in discussion with the author, January 2013.

22. Stephanie Coutu, in discussion with the author, October 2012.

23. Interview with attorney and high-tech executive, 2012. Name withheld by mutual agreement.

24. Wilford, interview.

25. Kaye A. Thomas, *Consider Your Options: Get the Most from Your Equity Compensation* (Lisle: Fairmark
     Press, 2000), 168–169.

26. John Pletz, "Good news-bad news scenarios for Groupon shares," *Crain's Chicago Business*, last updated
     June 1, 2012, accessed November 2, 2013, http://www.chicagobusiness.com/article/20120601/
     NEWS08/120539949/good-news-bad-news-scenarios-for-groupon-shares#.

27. Aaron Pressman, "Candy Crush Saga Could Be Far Better IPO Story Than Zynga," Yahoo! Finance,
     last updated September 27, 2013, accessed November 2, 2013, http://finance.yahoo.com/blogs/
     the-exchange/candy-crush-saga-could-far-better-ipo-story-190037091.html.

28. Interview with experienced executive at Silicon Valley companies, 2012. Name withheld by mutual
     agreement.

29. "Taxable and Nontaxable Income," Publication 525, Department of the Treasury, Internal Revenue
     Service, accessed August 7, 2012, http://www.irs.gov/pub/irs-pdf/p525.pdf.

30. Thomas, *Consider Your Options*, 188.

31. Thomas, *Consider Your Options*, 56.

32. Ken Goldman, in discussion with the author, March 2012.

33. Jason Graham, email message to author, December 17, 2013.

34. Graham, email message to author, December 27, 2013.

35. An SEC filing used by public companies to register their securities with the U.S. Securities and
     Exchange Commission (SEC) as the "registration statement by the Securities Act of 1933." The S-1
     contains the basic business and financial information on an issuer with respect to a specific securities
     offering.

36. "Publication 525 (2013), Taxable and Nontaxable Income," International Revenue
     Service, accessed January 26, 2013, http://www.irs.gov/publications/p525/ar02
     .html#en_US_2011_publink1000229243.

37. National Association of Tax Professionals, email message to author, January 9, 2013.

Phase 2: Ramping Up

1. Sonja Hoel Perkins, in discussion with the author, April 2012.

2. "Agilent Technologies Signs Agreement to Acquire Velocity11, a Leader in Life Science Lab
    Automation and Robotics," Agilent Technologies, last updated November 7, 2007, accessed
    January 5, 2014, http://www.agilent.com/about/newsroom/presrel/2007/07nov-gp07028.html.

3. Rob Nail, in discussion with the author, July 2012.

4. Interview with engineer and entrepreneur, 2012. Name withheld by mutual agreement.

5. Sylvia Yam, in discussion with the author, July 2012. Although permission was granted to utilize her quotes from 2012, she later expressed via email on January 2, 2014, that recent professional experiences altered her current opinions on these matters.

6. Interview with startup advisor, 2012. Name withheld by mutual agreement.

7. Jim Koshland, in discussion with the author, August 2012.

8. Jessica Guynn, "Facebook IPO: Mark Zuckerberg says 'Stay focused & keep shipping,'" *L.A. Times*, last updated February 1, 2012, accessed January 17, 2013, http://latimesblogs.latimes.com/technology/2012/02/facebook-ipo-mark-zuckerberg-stay-focused-keep-shipping.html.

9. Mark Zuckerberg, Facebook Mobile Uploads, last updated February 1, 2012, accessed January 17, 2013, https://www.facebook.com/photo.php?fbid=10100230247154651.

10. Conor Myhrvold, "Max Levchin," MIT *Technology Review*, last updated June 19, 2012, accessed August 7, 2012, http://www.technologyreview.com/qa/428186/max-levchin/.

11. "Form S-1 Registration Statement, Yelp! Inc.," United States Securities and Exchange Commission, last updated November 17, 2011, accessed January 7, 2014, http://www.sec.gov/Archives/edgar/data/1345016/000119312511315562/d245328ds1.htm#rom245328_14.

12. Deborah L. Jacobs, "How A Serial Entrepreneur Built A $95 Million Tax Free Roth IRA," *Forbes*, last updated March 20, 2012, accessed August 7, 2012, http://www.forbes.com/sites/deborahljacobs/2012/03/20/how-facebook-billionaires-dodge-mega-millions-in-taxes/.

13. Deborah L. Jacobs, "Why—And How—Congress Should Curb Roth IRAs," *Forbes*, last updated March 26, 2012, accessed August 17, 2012, http://www.forbes.com/sites/deborahljacobs/2012/03/26/why-and-how-congress-should-curb-roth-iras/.

14. Graham, email message to author, December 14, 2013.

15. Jacobs, "How A Serial Entrepreneur Built A $95 Million Tax Free Roth IRA." http://www.forbes.com/sites/deborahljacobs/2012/03/20/how-facebook-billionaires-dodge-mega-millions-in-taxes/.

16. Loren Feldman, "Goldman Sachs and the $580 Million Black Hole," *New York Times*, last updated July 14, 2012, accessed July 26, 2012, http://www.nytimes.com/2012/07/15/business/goldman-sachs-and-a-sale-gone-horribly-awry.html?pagewanted=all&_r=1&.

17. Ibid.

18. Ibid.

19. Ibid.

20. Marlee Myers, in discussion with the author, July 2012.

21 Marlee Myers, email message to author, December 20, 2013.

22. Lara Druyan, in discussion with the author, October 2012.

23. Brendan Richardson, in discussion with the author, April 2012.

24. Mark Cameron White, in discussion with the author, April 2012.

25. Beth L. Kramer, Esq., email message to author, February 6, 2014.

Liquidity Event: The Payoff

1. Interview with serial entrepreneur, 2012. Name withheld by mutual agreement.

2. John Bowen, in discussion with the author, February 2012.

3. "Borg (*Star Trek*)," *Wikipedia*, accessed November 6, 2012, http://en.wikipedia.org/wiki/Borg_%28Star_Trek%29.

4. Interview with entrepreneur and executive, 2012. Name withheld by mutual agreement.

5. Whittaker, "Why I left Google," http://blogs.msdn.com/b/jw_on_tech/archive/2012/03/13/why-i-left-google.aspx.

6. Paul Buchheit, "Communicating with code," last updated January 22, 2009, accessed January 4, 2014, http://paulbuchheit.blogspot.com/2009/01/communicating-with-code.html.

7. Lise Buyer, in discussion with the author, January 2012.

8. Interview with marketing executive, 2012. Name withheld by mutual agreement.

9. Rebecca Weeks Watson, in discussion with the author, November 2011.

10. Rebecca Weeks Watson, email message to author, November 28, 2013.

11. Interview with financial services executive, 2012. Name withheld by mutual agreement.

Phase 3: Realizing the Dream

1. Watson, email message to author, November 28, 2013.

2. David Goldman, "Welcome TSLA: Tesla Motors raises $266 million in IPO," CNNMoney.com, last updated June 29, 2010, accessed November 2, 2013, http://money.cnn.com/2010/06/29/technology/tesla_ipo/.

3. "Company Overview of NuvoMedia, Inc.," *Bloomberg Businessweek*, accessed November 2, 2013, http://investing.businessweek.com/research/stocks/private/snapshot.asp?privcapId=32306.

4. Martin Eberhard, in discussion with the author, February 2012.

5. Martin Eberhard, LinkedIn profile page, accessed March 2, 2012, http://www.linkedin.com/pub/martin-eberhard/1/193/144.

6. "Networking, Storage & Telecommunications," Foundation Capital, accessed November 21, 2013, http://www.foundationcapital.com/portfolio/networking-storage-telecommunications.php.

7. Jim Milliot and Steven Zeitchik, "Gemstar Acquires NuvoMedia, SoftBook," last updated January 24, 2000, accessed August 2, 2014, http://www.publishersweekly.com/pw/print/20000124/18802-pw-gemstar-acquires-nuvomedia-softbook.html.

8. "Tesla Motors, Inc. Stock Chart," Yahoo! Finance, accessed January 8, 2014, http://finance.yahoo.com/echarts?s=TSLA+Interactive#symbol=tsla;range=5y;compare=;indicator=split+dividend+volume;charttype=line;crosshair=on;ohlcvalues=0;logscale=off;source=undefined.

9. Scott Thurm, "Schmidt to Sell Google Stake Worth $2.5 Billion," *Wall Street Journal*, last updated February 8, 2013, accessed February 9, 2013, http://online.wsj.com/article/SB10001424127887324590904578292541060345994.html?mod=WSJ_article_comments#articleTabs%3Darticle.

10. Ibid.

11. Ibid.

12. Interview with attorney and high-tech executive, 2012. Name withheld by mutual agreement.

13. Interview with high-tech executive, 2012. Name withheld by mutual agreement.

14. Interview with business development executive, 2012. Name withheld by mutual agreement.

15. "Company Overview of NuvoMedia, Inc.," *Bloomberg Businessweek*.

16. Robert Carter, in discussion with the author, April 2012.

17. Robert Carter, email message to author, July 3, 2013.

18. Ibid.

19. David McCann, "Severance Severed for Ex-Gemstar Chief," *CFO*, last updated April 9, 2008, accessed July 31, 2012, http://www.cfo.com/article.cfm/11015765/c_11003041. Stephen Taub, "Gemstar Ex-CEO Ordered to Pay $22 Million," *CFO*, last updated May 9, 2006, accessed July 31, 2012, http://www.cfo.com/article.cfm/6907979.

20. Interview with business development executive, 2012. Name withheld by mutual agreement.

21. Interview with business development executive, 2012. Name withheld by mutual agreement.

22. Interview with entrepreneur and executive, 2012. Name withheld by mutual agreement.

23. Ibid.

24. Ibid.

25. Ibid.

26. Eric Gold, LinkedIn profile page, accessed July 9, 2012, http://www.linkedin.com/in/ericgold.

27. Jay Yarow, "How Google Dealt With Everyone Suddenly Getting Rich Thanks To An IPO," *Business Insider*, last updated May 16, 2012, accessed January 17, 2013, http://www.businessinsider.com/how-google-dealt-with-everyone-suddenly-getting-rich-thanks-to-an-ipo-2012-5#ixzz2IGXXzqs9.

28. Ibid.

29. Interview with engineer, 2012. Name withheld by mutual agreement.

30. "Whipsaw," *Investopedia*, accessed February 9, 2013, http://www.investopedia.com/terms/w/whipsaw.asp#axzz2KQETRdSO.

31. The decision tree graphic was made using an Excel add-in made by TreePlan Software (http://www.treeplan.com). For more information, see http://www.treeplan.com/treeplan-for-decision-trees.htm.

32. Interview with executive, 2012. Name withheld by mutual agreement.

33. Certified Financial Planner Board of Standards, Inc., *What You Should Know About Financial Planning* (CFP Board, 2009).

34. Ken Goldman, in discussion with the author, March 2012.

35. Excerpted from the book *The Investment Answer: Learn to Manage Your Money & Protect Your Financial Future* by Daniel C. Goldie, CFA, CFP® & Gordon S. Murray. Copyright © 2011 by Daniel C. Goldie and Gordon S. Murray. Reprinted by permission of Business Plus. All rights reserved.

36. James Picerno, "Weights and Bands," *Wealth Manager* (2007), accessed October 25, 2012.

37. New research from Morningstar shows that compared to a DIY investor, the added value of financial planning can be an extra 1.82% per year to investment returns. See Returns of DIY Investors, page 116.

38. Interview with business development executive, 2012. Name withheld by mutual agreement.

39. Interview with high-tech executive, 2012. Name withheld by mutual agreement.

40. Roccy DeFrancesco, "2012 DALBAR Study Reveals Average Investor Returns," *Physician's Money Digest*, last updated April 20, 2012, accessed September 29, 2012, http://www .physiciansmoneydigest.com/personal-finance/2012-DALBAR-Study.

41. DALBAR 2012 Quantitative Analysis of Investor Behavior (QAIB) study.

42. Returns data from the DALBAR 2012 Quantitative Analysis of Investor Behavior (QAIB) study.

43. Chuck Jaffe, "Are financial advisers worth their fee?," MarketWatch, last updated September 26, 2012, accessed October 23, 2012, http://www.marketwatch.com/story/ are-financial-advisers-worth-their-fee-2012-09-26.

44. Interview with executive, 2012. Name withheld by mutual agreement.

45. Jeff Russakow, in discussion with the author, March 2012.

46. Jeff Russakow, email message to author, November 26, 2013.

47. Interview with entrepreneur and executive, 2012. Name withheld by mutual agreement.

48. Nilene R. Evans, *Frequently Asked Questions about Rule 10b5-1 Plans* (San Francisco: Morrison & Foerster LLP, 2010).

49. Ibid.

50. For illustrative purposes only. Performance data shown represents past performance. Past performance is no guarantee of future results and current performance may be higher or lower than the performance shown. Average annual total returns include reinvestment of dividends and capital gains. The principal risk in investing may include one or more of the following: market risk, foreign securities and currencies risk, and interest rate risk. Results are net of fees and expenses. Indices are not available for direct investment. Full descriptions of indices used above are located in the Sources section on page 185.

51. For illustrative purposes only. Performance data shown represents past performance. Past performance is no guarantee of future results and current performance may be higher or lower than the performance shown. Average annual total returns include reinvestment of dividends and capital gains. The principal risk in investing may include one or more of the following: market risk, foreign securities and currencies risk, and interest rate risk. Results are net of fees and expenses. Indices are not available for direct investment. Full descriptions of indices used above are located in the Sources section on page 185.

Phase 4: What's Next?

1. Druyan, interview.

2. Ben Heskett, "Extreme climbs following strong IPO," *CNET*, last updated April 9, 1999, accessed November 2, 2013, http://news.cnet.com/Extreme-climbs-following-strong-IPO/ 2100-1033_3-224195.html.

3. Interview with advisor, 2012. Name withheld by mutual agreement.

4. Email message from CEO to author, December 21, 2013. Name withheld by mutual agreement.

5. Interview with CEO, 2012. Name withheld by mutual agreement.

6. Interview with serial entrepreneur, 2012. Name withheld by mutual agreement.

7. Richard Pivnicka, in discussion with the author, January 2012.

8. Matt Miller, "Movers and shakers: Remembering Warren Hellman," *Deal*, last updated January 20, 2012, accessed July 30, 2012, http://www.thedeal.com/magazine/ID/044059/2012/movers-and-shakers:-remembering-warren-hellman.php (link discontinued).

9. Joe Eskenazi, "Warren Hellman, Incidental Banjo Player," *SF Weekly*, last updated December 23, 2011, accessed July 31, 2012, http://blogs.sfweekly.com/thesnitch/2011/12/warren_hellman_banjo.php?print=true.

10. Miller, "Movers and shakers: Remembering Warren Hellman."

11. Jeffrey Skoll, *Forbes* profile, last updated September 2013, accessed January 6, 2014, http://www.forbes.com/profile/jeffrey-skoll/.

12. Interview with Silicon Valley connector, 2012. Name withheld by mutual agreement.

13. Interview with financial services executive, 2012. Name withheld by mutual agreement.

14. "Yahoo! Inc. 2012 Form 10-K," United States Securities and Exchange Commission, accessed November 2, 2013, http://www.sec.gov/Archives/edgar/data/1011006/000119312513085111/d442073d10k.htm.

15. "Excite@Home—Excite, 1994–1998," Net Industries, accessed November 2, 2013, http://ecommerce.hostip.info/pages/434/Excite-Home-EXCITE-1994-1998.html.

16. "Fortinet IPO soars on opening day," *Silicon Valley Business Journal*, last updated November 18, 2009, accessed November 2, 2013, http://www.bizjournals.com/sanjose/stories/2009/11/16/daily45.html?page=all.

17. Stephen Roth, in discussion with the author, June 2012.

18. Jason Zasky, "Fool's Gold? Debunking the Myths of Angel Investing," *Failure Magazine*, accessed July 24, 2012, http://failuremag.com/feature/article/fools_gold/.

19. Nicolai Wadstrom, in discussion with the author, July 2012.

20. Nicolai Wadstrom, email message to author, November 27, 2013.

21. Darrell Kong, in discussion with the author, February 2012.

Partnering with an Advisor at Any Phase

1. John Bowen, email message to author, December 20, 2013.

2. Bowen, email message to author, October 9, 2013.

3. Tim Sobolewski, "Fiduciary vs. Suitability—Which standard is best?," Financial Planning Association, last updated September 25, 2012, accessed October 9, 2013, http://www.fpanet.org/ToolsResources/ArticlesBooksChecklists/Articles/FinancialPlanning/FiduciaryvsSuitabilityWhichstandardisbest/ (link discontinued).

4. Interview with advisor, 2012. Name withheld by mutual agreement.

5. Interview with entrepreneur and CEO, 2012. Name withheld by mutual agreement.

6. "Experience Requirement," CFP Board, accessed September 9, 2013, http://www.cfp.net/become-a-cfp-professional/cfp-certification-requirements/experience-requirement.

7. Mark P. Cussen, "CFP*, CLU or ChFC—Which Is Best?," *Investopedia*, accessed October 23, 2012, http://www.investopedia.com/articles/professionaleducation/08/cfp-clu-chfc.asp.

8. "Fiduciary Oath," NAPFA, accessed September 9, 2013, http://www.napfa.org/about/FiduciaryOath.asp.

Appendix

1. Richard Pivnicka biography, provided during discussion with the author, April 2010.

2. "Mitch Kapor: BLC Business Leadership Breakfast Keynote Speech," YouTube video, from a speech entitled "From Gold to Good: Innovating a Better World" given at the Jewish Community Federation & Endowment Fund Business Leadership Breakfast on May 16, 2012, posted by "sfjcf," May 31, 2012, http://www.youtube.com/watch?v=Un5r8Z5_wpA.

3. Mitch Kapor, email message to author, August 5, 2012.

INDEX